MW00461874

Mike «C-ROC» Ciorrocco

ROCKET FUEL

Convert Setbacks.
Become Unstoppable.

ROCKET FUEL

Rocket Fuel
Convert Setbacks. Become Unstoppable.

www.mikecroc.com

Disclaimer
This book contains the ideas and opinions of its author. The intention of this book is to provide information, helpful content, and motivation to readers about the subjects addressed. Although every precaution has been taken to verify the accuracy of the information contained herein, the author and publisher assume no responsibility for any errors or omissions. The intent of this author is only to offer suggestions to help the reader in the quest for organizing their personal affairs. The author and publisher urge readers to seek professional legal counsel and appropriate expert advice.

No warranties or guarantees are expressed or implied by the author's choice to include any of the content in this volume. The author shall not be liable for any physical, psychological, emotional, financial, or commercial damages, including, but not limited to, special, incidental, consequential, or other damages. The reader is responsible for their own choices, actions, and results.

1st Edition. 1st printing 2021

Cover Concept and Design: Antonio White
Interior Design: Steve Walters
Editors: Jean-Pierre Martel, Richard Tardif
Editors: Chip Hopper, Brooke Heym
Photography: Photo of Mike Ciorrocco by Dorian Ash

Independently Published
Oxygen Publishing Inc.
2515, rue Dutrisac
Vaudreuil-Dorion, QC, Canada J7V 9W7
www.oxygenpublishing.com

ISBN: 978-1-0879-1169-4

Why Rocket Fuel?

Are you ready? I've discovered a way to become unstoppable and indestructible. I've found it's possible to convert setbacks, letdowns, difficulties, and criticism into **ROCKET FUEL** to launch yourself to new heights and to become unstoppable and indestructible.

I call it "**ROCKET FUEL**" because rocket fuel is the only source I know of that can propel you out of Earth's gravitational pull and put you into orbit and beyond - even if fuel stinks like hell and is toxic and nasty. In life, gravity is a suppressor. It's something that pulls you down and keeps you from moving forward, towards your goals and dreams. **ROCKET FUEL** has the rare ability to ignite your inner strength and take you into orbit, away from the pull of gravity.

What does "orbit and beyond" look like to you?

What do you need that would put you beyond orbit?

You need **FUEL** to give you **THRUST**.

THRUST is a **MUST**.

THRUST comes from **ABUNDANCE**.

It comes from the abundance of whatever it is that allows you to wake up every day and do what you "want to do" instead of what you "have to do."

To some it's money.

To others it may be doing a job or activity that makes them happy.

What is it to you?

What is it that stops you from getting what you want?

It's not the wins, the encouraging/supportive people, or the targets you hit that stop you from getting what you want. What is stopping you from getting what you want are the setbacks, the letdowns, the difficulties, and the negative people.

ROCKET FUEL

What if the things you saw as holding you back were instead propelling you forward? What if you could use those things as **ROCKET FUEL**?

What would your life look like? Is that a life you would want?

The important part is to learn to be proactive in this mindset.

By grasping this concept NOW and moving forward, you can start to look for the things that stop or slow you down, and know that they are needed for fuel to give you thrust.

Now when you experience a suppressor, it will propel you.

This gives you a huge advantage over anyone else that doesn't live by this concept.

By choosing to read this book, you have decided to embark on a wonderful journey into space – your space – that will allow you to discover the immense power of converting setbacks into fuel, thrusting you towards your most fantastic goals, and capable of converting mistakes into great possibilities.

Based on my own humble experience, I plan to tell you how to launch your fantastic self on a wonderful, successful journey into orbit and beyond.

There was a time when I thought I knew everything.

In fact, it wasn't too long ago that my ego was running me. I approached life as if I knew things when I should have been spending more time in thankfulness and absorbing knowledge.

As Mike Tyson says, "Adversity makes the strong stronger and the weak weaker."

As you read, could you do me a favor?

Make a commitment to yourself to have an open mind and take what you learn here and implement it.

One of the things I find most tragic in this world is that people fail to take action on the information they receive, even when it could drastically improve their lives.

In the following chapters, I'll share experiences on how I've used **ROCKET FUEL** to propel me through tough times and setbacks, to break down barriers, and to reach my goals.

I know **ROCKET FUEL** can work for you too.

Foreword
by Grant Cardone

There is one thing that you are guaranteed to encounter in your business, your relationships, literally every area of your life… and how you respond will determine the level of success that you will achieve.

So what is the thing I am referring to? Setbacks.

Imagine if you had the super power of recovering better, stronger and smarter after every setback?

I have experienced enormous setbacks in my life. More than most and not nearly as many as others.

But my life has been riddled with setbacks, hardships, letdowns, disappointments, and even tragedy, that most people don't even know about.

First, I lost my dad at 10 years old, was bullied through my high school years, lost my older brother in my twenties, was beaten to within inches of my life at 23, had a life-threatening drug problem, took me three years in my first business to make money, and I almost went bankrupt. All of that was before I turned 30.

The reason I am telling you this is because many of those setbacks and hardships are the reason I am where I am today. When you learn how to convert setbacks into springboards, they can become **ROCKET FUEL** for your success.

I could have quit 10,000 times in my life…. but I didn't.

I continued to show up. I continued to take action despite the disappointments, discouragements and at times despair.

The important thing was that I did just that. I kept showing up.

ROCKET FUEL

After every failure, after every setback, after every letdown, I continued to show up and look for how the setback had made me more resilient.

I wish I could tell you that after time, things get easy and the setbacks will go away, but they don't. In fact, they grow in size, and that is why if you want any chance at doing something remarkable, you must start today to look at setbacks not as obstacles, but as an indication that you are on the right track. **You must learn to convert the losses into ROCKET FUEL.**

That's why I am so excited for you to read, **ROCKET FUEL**. Convert Setbacks. Become Unstoppable, where Mike gives you concrete examples and steps to follow to ensure that you can take what most people treat as a liability and convert disappointment, discouragement and even the desire to quit into one of your most powerful assets. Once you learn from this book how to convert setbacks into **ROCKET FUEL** you will become unstoppable and your success will be all but guaranteed.

ROCKET FUEL is for You!

Grant Cardone

Dedication

*This book is dedicated to all of those that
believed in me from day one and to those that
attempted to discourage and/or gave up on me.*

You have been and continue to be my ROCKET FUEL.

ROCKET FUEL

Acknowledgements

To all those who have been instrumental in inspiring my **ROCKET FUEL** journey, many of you are in this book, and I must thank you each individually.

To my Dad who lit a fire in me at a young age.

To my Mom, who programmed me at a young age to be a leader and one that would inspire others.

To my late stepfather, George, for showing me how to be a man that always shows up.

To my wife, Jen, and my children, Nicolas and Sophia you are my everything.

To my business partners and best friends Chris Short, Jason Yates, Beau Cox, and my little Bro Casey Holland: I thank you for holding down the fort for me while I went out and got us set up for our next several huge missions.

To Kim Lee for keeping me on the right track and making sure that I don't miss anything.

To Brandon Dawson, Jarrod Glandt, and Richard Dolan thank you for the friendship, wisdom, and support that you provided as I started my journey to become UNSTOPPABLE.

To Greg Reid thank you for the work that you put into your career prior to meeting me so that you could pour the lessons that you learned into me and so many others.

To Bill Osbourne, Jeremy Sopko, and the rest of the Nations Lending Family thank you for the support you have given not only to me but also to my team.

ROCKET FUEL

To Antonio White, a.k.a. The Pitchfreak, thank you for your friendship, advice, and the absolutely awesome cover design.

To Carolyn Flower for getting be started in the author journey and guiding me through the process of writing a book.

To JP Martel and Richard Tardif for cleaning up my brain dump.

To Chip Hopper and Brooke Heym for coming in late in the game to tighten up my manuscript and investing so many hours. Thank you!!

To Grant and Elena Cardone, you two have set the example for so many of us that were looking for "The Way". Thank you! G, we are all chasing you and the best part about having you as a mentor is that you are always raising the bar to stay way ahead of us.

Chapters Counting Down to Liftoff

"*A journey of a thousand miles begins with a single step.*" - Lao Tzu

"*We need to break through broken mindsets*" - Brandon Dawson

"*Become Unstoppable and Indestructible*" - Grant Cardone

"*Spend a lifetime learning.*" - Richard Dolan

"*You Need Clear Skies to Launch for The Stars.*" - Jarrod Glandt

"*Culture isn't just one aspect of the game, it is the game. In the end, an organization is nothing more than the collective capacity of its people to create value.*" - Lou Gerstner

"*Communication is Everything*" - Jen Ciorrocco

"*Refuse to be the victim.*" - Avery Warner

CHAPTER 17

My Story, The Countdown Begins

*"A journey of a thousand miles begins
with a single step."* - Lao Tzu

A Pretty Normal Life

I don't remember my parents together other than in wedding pictures. They got divorced when I was only a few months old. Growing up I thought I had a normal life and that every kid went to his dad's house every other weekend.

As a dad now, I realize how hard it must have been for my parents to be in that situation.

There was always a lot of conflict over custody, child support, as well as jealousy from my stepmother towards me, my mother, and my dad's side of the family.

I know now that this conflict was not targeted at me personally, but it sure did feel like it back then and it conditioned me to be calloused to conflict and uncomfortable situations.

I was the oldest of all the grandchildren on both sides of my family. The first grandchild is always such a novelty and some of my earliest memories are of my aunts, uncles, and grandparents being so excited anytime I was around. I remember getting so much attention and admiration (and love, yes!).

But I felt this attention and love dwindle as more children and grandchildren were born into the family.

Back And Forth

I often spent my dad-weekends at his parents' house because my dad worked all the time. He was a mason and masons need to take advantage of working whenever the weather is good. Living with my mom, we would move to different apartments regularly.

My mom worked and I spent that time at a daycare center called the Pied Piper. When I was around two, I was left unsupervised and ended up getting into a huge tub of Vaseline. So much for my awesome head of curly hair!

I remember there was an old man who worked at The Pied Piper that everyone called Uncle John. Uncle John had a strong Greek accent and a short temper. He would often pull off his belt and light us up with it when he felt we were acting up.

Around age five, my mom remarried a man named Larry and they had a daughter, my sister Kim. After five years of being an only child with a single mom, I suddenly had a new father figure and a new baby sister. It was uncomfortable at times, but kids are resilient and I figured my way through it.

Like many siblings do, my sister Kimmy and I had our fights , but we were close and, for the most part, had a great relationship.

From what I remember, Larry and I got along great as well. He was a big Philadelphia Eagles fan, which is something we had in common. Larry wasn't around long. My mom and Larry got divorced shortly after Kim was born. Now it was just me, Mom, and Kim.

Times were tough for my mom as a single parent with two young children. We had to switch daycares and ended up in a dark and musty daycare in our apartment complex. It was miserable. I dreaded going there every day. I can still recall the feeling of being trapped and being held prisoner. This is the earliest memory of feeling a lack of control and of being stuck in a position because of someone's else's problems.

*Those early experiences of having no control
fueled my desire to put myself in situations I can control.*

Here We Go

When I was about eight years old, my mom met a man at work named George.

George was a no-nonsense, black-and-white kind of guy.

He was a true outdoorsman - hunting and fishing for everything.

I remember the first time we went to George's house. The drive felt like days. There was nothing to see but woods and farmland and brown corn stalks standing high along the roads as my mom drove us to the middle of nowhere, also known as Earleville, Maryland. George's place was a little two-bedroom bungalow. I remember walking in for the first time, not knowing what to expect. The place smelled like deer piss and fishing lures. There was old-time country music playing on a small radio and an old, stained reclining chair with a bunch of North American Whitetail and Bass Master magazines.

I remember thinking, "What in the heck are we supposed to do here?"

My mom and George got married. I was not a real fan of George in the beginning. He was a hard man and I wasn't used to a lot of discipline. I couldn't wrap my head around the idea of my mom bringing a second father figure into my life. I assumed my dad was aware of what was going on. I don't remember specifics, but I do remember there being a lot of conflict over child support payments. I don't know how my dad felt, but I assume he had strong opinions about who my mom was bringing into my life and about paying child support. I always felt I was in the middle of the arguments.

*Money became a frequent topic on my mind at a young age and
I decided early on that I would figure out a way that finances
would not be a problem for me and my family when I grew up.*

ROCKET FUEL

One weekend after finding out we were moving in with George, my dad took me out to dinner. He took me to my favorite restaurant, a little Italian restaurant in Wilmington, Delaware called Mrs. Robino's. It smelled like cigarettes and garlic and was a dark, smoky joint like you see in mob movies, but it was my favorite restaurant because of its cheese ravioli.

My dad had this plan to sell me on the idea of moving in with him full time, probably because he was trying to get out of child support. As I sat and ate my dinner that night at the restaurant, it was like a timeshare sales pitch. My dad told me that if I came to live with him he would get me a puppy, a pool, and my own room with a waterbed. It was all the things a little kid would be enamored by. He reminded me I wouldn't have those things if I stayed living at my mom's house.

I Want To Move In With Dad

I guess I'm an easy sell. I went back to my mom's and broke the news. "I want to move in with Dad," I said with conviction. "I need a change and I'm not a fan of George. He is mean and hard on me."

I remember her being shocked. However, she gave me my wish without a fight. My parent time switched to only seeing my mom every other weekend. She later told me she cried herself to sleep at night for months after I left.

At first, my time at my dad's was great. I was the ring bearer at his huge, fancy wedding. I became famous at the reception when the DJ put on Michael Jackson's Billy Jean. I had watched the MTV video enough times that I thought I could perform just like Michael. For years after the wedding, we still ran into people who would say, "You're the break dancer from the wedding!"

After moving in with my dad and my stepmom, every time I would come back from my mom's house my stepmom would interrogate me about the trip. There was a lot of jealousy from my stepmom and, as you can imagine, the conversations made me very uncomfortable.

As I write this, it still brings back feelings and emotions that make me sick to my stomach. I was a nine-year-old kid caught between immature adults fighting and hating each other. The things that were said about my mom were so spiteful! A young child should never have to hear those words about his mom. I always felt I was the cause of whatever they were mad about.

I was so confused.

I knew I wasn't doing anything to cause this, but I still felt responsible. I was the only reason my parents still had to be in contact. I thought everyone experienced this kind of abuse.

I felt like I didn't have anywhere to turn for fear that no one would believe me or that I would get into trouble for speaking up. I now know this is a common feeling in victims of abuse.

New Home, New Family

My dad had a stepdaughter who is three years younger than me. We became close and did almost everything together. My dad had two more daughters during those years. I helped take care of the older of the two, Chrissy, as a baby, including changing her diapers and whatever it took to help keep her occupied. I remember loving her so much. I didn't get to know the younger sister during the three years I was there.

My dad and stepmom continued to have bad fights, cursing at each other. The tension in the house was unreal. At times, the fighting would turn towards me and sometimes the derogatory remarks from my stepmom would turn towards my mom.

I felt like I was responsible for it all. I carried it as a heavy burden for many years. When my stepmom would explode, my dad would always wink at me and give me a thumbs up, like he had things under control. Like, don't worry, bud. She's just in a mood. Ride it out, man.

> *The thought would go through my mind all the time, that there was no way, as a man, that I would put up with this.*
> *I would stand up for my son.*
>
> *Nobody, including my future wife, would treat my son that way.*

It always amazed me that he didn't stand up for me. It would have gone a long way with me. I always thought "How could a tough mason be such a pushover?"

> *I learned that people should be treated the right way and you should always stand up for people, especially for your family.*

The conflict extended out to my dad's sisters and his mom (my aunts and grandmother). My stepmom seemed to have felt as if her daughter, my stepsister, was not being treated as well as I was by them. We would come home from a holiday or special occasion with them and we would all have to hear about how she couldn't stand my aunts or my grandmother. A lot of times it would escalate into a fight between her and my dad. My stepsister and I would hide in one of our bedrooms and just listen to the distant yelling.

My stepsister was young and this fighting had a significant impact on her. She was between the ages of three and five at the time. It's terrible that a kid of that age should be subjected to adult fighting. Again, this conflict was projected onto me by my stepmom as if it was my fault.

She would tear into me in anger about the situation, making derogatory statements and comments about my aunts and grandmother, and blaming me for being treated better than her daughter.

It got to the point we stopped going to family events. At one point, we were not seeing my dad's side of the family anymore.

This hurt. I had always been close to my aunts, cousins and especially my grandparents.

My grandparents felt crushed, not being able to visit their oldest grandchild. I never understood why my dad allowed this to happen. My grandparents were great people. They would do anything for anyone.

The Longest Ride Of My Life

My paternal grandfather drove a school bus at my elementary school. I rode a different bus but he would call to me to come see him on his bus as

I walked by. Since I was cut off from seeing him, I was scared to death that someone would see me if I interacted with him.

He would wave at me and tell me it was ok. I would ignore him and keep going to my bus.

It was tearing me apart. I could only imagine how it made him feel.

One time as I walked past his bus, I thought, enough is enough. I went onto his bus to see him. He had a bag of candy that my grandmother "smuggled" to me.

As a nine-year-old it seemed crazy to feel like I had to sneak around to see my family. I stayed on his bus a little too long and my bus ended up leaving without me. There were no cell phones back then, so I had to ride his bus until the end of his route when he could drop me off. I was so nervous about what was going to happen. That ride was one of the longest rides of my life.

When I finally got dropped off, my grandfather tried to explain the situation to my stepmom. She was furious because I hadn't arrived on my bus, but she was even more furious that I was seeing my grandfather.

That night I got the wooden spoon so bad it broke. That didn't stop the beating. The remaining part of the spoon was used to finish off the mission.

I was so confused about why it was wrong to see my family that I loved.

Around Christmas one year, I came home from my mom's house after celebrating the holiday with my mom's side of the family. I had received Christmas presents from my mom and my aunts, uncles, and grandparents.

When I got back to my dad's, the toys were taken away from me. I was told it wasn't fair that I had received gifts when my dad's other children hadn't.

How was I supposed to comprehend this in my 10 year old mind?

ROCKET FUEL

CHAPTER 16

Where The Drive Started

"We need to break through broken mindsets"
- Brandon Dawson

Moving Back To Mom's

I often had an anxious upset feeling in my stomach when driving back to my dad's house after spending the weekend at my mom's house. It wasn't because of the hilly roads in southeastern Pennsylvania, it was because I knew the interrogation that was coming from my stepmother. I dreaded being back in that toxic environment.

One weekend when my mom was driving me back to my dad's, she could tell I was struggling and asked me what was wrong. I was tired of just going along with the torment, the mental abuse, and the constant bashing of my mom, grandparents, and aunts. This was going to come to an end. I wasn't going to be kept away from the family I wanted to see.

When I shared with my mom what was going on, she said she had no idea. She told me that it's not normal for a kid to live in an environment like the one I was living in with my dad and stepmother and it wasn't ok. She said I had a choice. I could move back with her if I wanted, or stay in that environment.

Stick To Your Guns

My mom asked me if I was sure I wanted to move back with her. She said she would do what needed to be done with the courts, but she needed to be sure it was what I wanted and that I was committed to the idea. She knew I could be sold by my dad on the idea of staying. She knew the environment could get worse for me after they knew I wanted to leave, especially if I kept bouncing back and forth on the idea.

My mom said, "Anytime you believe in something you need to stick to your guns. Others will try to talk you out of what you believe, but you can't allow it."

That was a great lesson for me, and for you. When you believe in something, others will try to make you see it their way.

Or they may feel threatened by your advancement and want to nullify your success. They will make comments to chip away at you until you come back to their level.

One day when I got home from school, I was told to go to my room and that my dad would be there in a minute. I probably only sat there for five minutes, but it felt like five hours.

My dad came in with a legal envelope. He said, "What is this?"

I was scared to death. I knew the envelope held the suit my mom had filed to regain custody, but I just shrugged my shoulders.

He explained what was in the envelope and proceeded to explain to me that my mom and George did not have it that well and how much better it was at his house.

My dad was my hero. When I had been living primarily with my mom, I couldn't wait to see my dad every other weekend. He owned his own masonry business and was a hard worker. He had big forearms and rough hands. I always admired him for his hard work and the money he made from it. He used to carry around a rolled-up wad of hundred-dollar bills with a rubber band around it. He would always flash it and show it off to me. I thought it was so cool.

I was terrified of disappointing my dad and making the wrong decision. When it came to money, I thought my dad was always right.

Then I thought of what my mom had told me, "Stick to your guns!"

I told my dad "I've made up my mind and this is what I'm going to do."

It was so hard for me to do.

Keep in mind, I still had to live at my dad's house while the courts did their thing.

My dad pulled out the wad of cash, peeled off a hundred dollar bill, crumpled it up, threw it at me, and said, "Here, you'll need this when you are living on the streets with your mother!"

Talk about throwing gasoline on the fire.

My hero, my dad, had just given up on me. I felt like a fighter who just had his cornerman throw in the towel. At first, I felt a sense of terror.

After getting over the initial terror, it came to me that there was no way I would let him be right this time.

I was going to show him. I would blow past anything he had accomplished and more.

I was going to prove him wrong- no matter what it took. I was going to be a better father, husband, businessman, and person than he ever was.

I'm a stubborn person. At that moment, and many more times in my life, this liability has been an asset, a true superpower. It has helped me tremendously in my life. It has been ROCKET FUEL for me.

I committed to helping others in my situation. Remember, I thought my life was ordinary and that all kids were going through the same experiences as me

> *I committed to helping all those that had been given up on. I didn't know how I was going to do it. I just started trying to be a role model for the people that had been through something like I had. I wanted to show them that no matter where you came from, or what had been done to you, you could be great.*

In sports, school, and in everything I did, I always tried to be the best.

In my mind I believed everyone was watching me and I couldn't let them down. I would not let him win.

There were many court hearings after that day, and even times when they required me to sit with a child psychologist to determine if I was mature enough to decide where I wanted to live.

I remember the psychologist telling me how mature and intelligent I was and how they wished my parents would act more like me. This should provide you with a little bit of color on how everyone was behaving.

This experience was huge for me as I got older. Awkward moments and tough calls to be made were easy for me. I would think to myself, "Remember what you are made of. Look at what you've been through already. This is nothing compared to those times."

It's kind of crazy how such a traumatic experience, one no child should have to go through, would be so beneficial in preparing me for the rest of my life.

Life isn't easy. None of us are immune to tough times. We all have to deal with crazy people and being treated unfairly.

I converted these times into ROCKET FUEL for my future.

Lessons From The Past

Whether we see it or not, all successful people use things from their past to continue to elevate and propel them forward on their journey to greatness.

I don't share the stories about my dad to tear him down. I'm far from perfect, and I have no room to judge. If I saw my dad today, I would give him a big hug and tell him I love him.

I share this story with you because this is a point in my life where I could have played the victim role. Instead, I chose to use it to light a huge fire inside of me that could not be put out. I chose to use these experiences as ROCKET FUEL for the rest of my life. These experiences are now allowing me to change the world and impact millions of people.

It took me until I was almost 40 to become clear on the fact that I had made use of these circumstances all my life. I'm now aware of leaning into this superpower to take full advantage of it. I now realize the massive number of people I have helped and influenced because of this. There are also many more I can help and influence going forward. I know I can inspire others to do the same with their stories.

If you've been in similar situations or times where you felt your world fell apart, I can show you how to use that as ROCKET FUEL to achieve greatness.

What events have occurred in your life?
Are you using them to hold you back?

Are you using one or more of them to justify playing the victim role?

I want you to pivot from any of those events towards lighting a fire in you.

It is ok if you started off using it in a negative manner or if you chose the wrong road. You can change it today. Make the change now; don't wait any longer. Make the commitment to yourself.

Get in a quiet place where you can think clearly.

ROCKET FUEL

On a piece of paper, write down the earliest setback event in your life that you can remember.

- Paint the picture.
- Put down as much detail as you can remember.
- How old were you?
- Where were you?
- Who was around. Who was involved?
- Why did it happen?
- How did it make you feel?

Now move forward from that point in your life to events and actions that people made that stand out in your mind. Events that made you feel either very good or very bad. Don't worry about the ones in the middle or the ones that don't stand out.

Write these down with as much detail as you can come up with. Work your way all the way back to the present.

The next step is where the magic happens. Start at the beginning Write down the lessons you learned and the values you gained from each event. If not a lesson or value, perhaps something someone did to you that you want to use to fuel your future. For clarification, I recommend against using spite as fuel. It will only consume you and it will take energy from your mission.

I want you to relate the lesson or the value to how you can use it now and in the future. Remember, these events can help you handle and get through tough times, setbacks, and relationship issues.

For example, when I was a kid and my parents were going through custody court battles, it was awkward for me to be around my dad and my stepmom after I decided to move out of their house. I couldn't stand it. I would start to sweat, and my stomach would be in knots.

Using the above exercise, I'm able to stroll calmly into situations that would be awkward for most people. I enter these situations thinking, "This is nothing compared to those court dates!"

Going forward, you will not necessarily use all these things.

You may use some of your events as fuel all the time and others may be used only at specific times.

The bottom line is, you need to move these events from the trunk where they weigh you down to the tank where you can use them as ROCKET FUEL. When you do, your life, and the events of your future, will become easier to handle.

> *However, my take on it is that I don't want things to be easier just to be easier. I want to find out how I can accomplish more and not be stopped or slowed down.*

The court decided I could live with my mom for the summer and then choose where I wanted to stay for the school year.

I moved back to Maryland with my mom and my stepdad, George, in the summer before my sixth grade year.

Lessons From Football

Peewee football camp started that summer. August 15 was the first day of practice.

Football was always a sport I loved and yearned to play. This was my first opportunity to have a taste of the action. I had no idea what I was getting myself into.

The first few practices were with no equipment. They were all about conditioning.

At eleven-years-old I hadn't trained for anything physically. I had no reference to know about pacing myself. I always went hard at anything I did.

So, when they told us to run, I sprinted. When they told us to jump, I tried to grab the clouds. Doing this without understanding that I needed to have enough energy to get through a two-hour practice just about killed me. I literally couldn't catch my breath and was quickly overheated. I learned a valuable lesson.

> *Not all scenarios require you to go all out, all at once.*
>
> *It pays to be calculated and, at times, to pace yourself.*

Nevertheless, I couldn't get enough of football.

We started adding equipment and started tackling at practice. That's when the contact came into play. Wow, now I had a way to get some of my past aggressions out of me that I couldn't before.

Being new to the game, I didn't know all of the rules. During one of our first practice games, called a scrimmage, I was hitting people from behind and knocking them down. They were falling so easily. I thought I was doing something great. Of course this is against the rules.

During a long-running play where one of my teammates scored a touchdown, the referee threw a yellow flag saying there was a penalty. The touchdown was called back because of the penalty against me for hitting someone from behind. Everyone was so upset with me.

I let the team down.

I had no idea until the coach started yelling at me, letting me know the rule right in the heat of the battle.

> *The lesson from this was, know what you are doing.*
>
> *Not knowing something is no excuse.*
>
> *Study, learn, ALWAYS.*
>
> *If you don't, you can and will let your team down.*

Thankfully I did redeem myself that game. I scored four touchdowns as a running back. I was on top of the world and thought I was the next Walter Payton. However, throughout the rest of my football career of nine years, I only scored one other touchdown!

> *The lesson I learned from that experience was to stay humble.*

I made some great friends in high school. We had a football team that never had enough players to fully practice.

As much as we loved playing on both sides of the ball, if someone got hurt we had no one to replace them. No matter what team we played, we were always the smaller, slower team with the least number of players. Somehow though, our high school team won more than half our games.

We had to rely on something other than endurance and athletic ability. We had to be smarter and grittier.

We developed an underdog mentality.

During the pee wee football days, we had never won a game. We took that mentality with us to high school and played like we had nothing to lose anytime we stepped on the field. Teams that were not prepared and took us for granted got smacked in the mouth.

From my sophomore year on, I started as an outside linebacker. I was quite good at reading the offense. That made up for my lack of size and speed, allowing me to be a step ahead of the offensive-line players.

In our senior year, we won seven games and made the playoffs for the first time.

It was a huge deal for us.

We gained confidence that year, one game at a time. We started stacking the wins and, after each one, we began to develop a little swagger. By the time we were halfway through the season, we thought we could take on anyone.

During that playoff game, we were winning with about a minute to go. For some reason, our coach called in a pass play. Our quarterback threw an interception and on the next play the other team scored the winning touchdown.

We were crushed.

> *Lesson, it's not over until it's over.*
> *Be smarter and grittier. FINISH!*

Despite that loss, that season had a huge impact on our confidence in life. It also developed a bond that would last a lifetime among our teammates.

Football stayed my passion all the way through two years of college football.

Playing the game taught me so many lessons for life and business. It taught me discipline, commitment, leadership, communication, effort, and the value of goal setting, to name a few.

A Diamond In The Rough

Back to the sixth grade and being the new kid in my elementary school.

In my old school, most of the kids in my class were Latino, so most of my friends were Latino.

Unlike my old school, I noticed in my new school that there was a division between minority kids and white kids. I had never paid much attention to race before and had always gotten along with everyone.

I tried to make new friends at my new school and I got my ass whooped. Apparently I needed to be broken into the group. One night at the school, I went up to the second floor to get my coat after a music concert. There were no adults up there. There were, however, three or four kids who started beating on me. I had never been in a situation like that. I was confused because I hadn't had any issues with these kids before. As they beat me up, they were laughing like it was a game.

No one came to my rescue. When I was finally able to get away, I ran back down to the first floor. My mom saw the tears streaming down my face and inquired hysterically what had happened.

I was afraid to tell her, but another kid who had seen what happened told her.

She hit the ceiling. She hunted down the principal and demanded that she get the kids in a room together. When that finally happened, she tore into them.

She made it clear that I always got along with everyone and that there was no reason for what had taken place to happen.

I was so embarrassed.

Here she was standing up for me, but I was more concerned with what the kids were thinking and what was going to happen the next day in school. One thing I knew was that if it ever happened again, I was going to fight back and punish at least one of the attackers.

I was never going to let that happen again.

That event prompted me to react to anyone instigating something with me. From that point on, all the way through college, if someone started what I thought was going to end up in an altercation, I just hit them first.

Our school was so small that we moved to high school in the seventh grade. I was again in a brand new environment with kids from seventh grader through twelfth grade. Being picked on and bullied was common, but I didn't take it from anyone. I got in several fights.

I never got suspended from school because I had a great reputation as a student and the kids I fought with were labelled as bad kids. When I went to the principal's office, I would sell Principal Dr. Jackson on my case. I would paint the picture and ask him what he would have done if he were in the same situation. That always got me out of suspension. Instead he had me write papers on why fighting is not good and what I thought I could have done differently.

Looking back, I'm thankful he didn't give up on me.

Dr. Jackson saw something in me that he could work with. Even with the fighting, I focused on being the best student I could be.

I'm not proud of some of the things I did. There were times I could have walked away or talked my way out of it, but, with the trauma that comes from being jumped, I never wanted to take that chance. I thought this behavior would make a statement and that less people would be inclined to start something with me.

ROCKET FUEL

Luckily, I was never arrested and never hurt anyone too badly.

ROCKET FUEL Origins

Not only was I having a hard time with the transition to the new school, I was also having a hard time at home. I was trying to get used to living in another man's house, along with constant reminders of what I had given up leaving my dad's.

My stepmom was constantly sending mail with pictures of vacations, holidays, and presents that had been given to my siblings. The letters included were written as if they were coming from my sisters. However, you could tell by how they were written that there was more of a motive behind it. It was deliberately done to rub it in my face.

My dad and stepmom ended up having a son. They gave him the same middle name as my first name, which is the same as my dad's name.

In the letters, instead of calling him by his first name, they would say, "Michael this" and. "Michael that."

It was absolutely insane.

> *Instead of letting it bother me, I used it as*
> *ROCKET FUEL for my future.*

I raised my intensity in school and sports. I kept telling myself, "I'll show them!"

I always operated like my dad could see everything I was doing.

During that sixth-grade year, I met three guys who would become my business partners twenty years later. One in particular, Chris Short, instantly hit it off with me. He ended up being the best man at my wedding. Chris played pee wee football too. Chris was an exceptionally good football player. He had heard of me prior to meeting me because of the four-touchdown game I had. In his best man speech at my wedding, he said he was concerned I was going to steal the spotlight from him. He told me that the first time he saw me he thought, "That's him? He's nothing to worry about."

> *That is a lesson in itself.*
>
> *We get these images and thoughts in our heads a lot of times in the worst-case scenario. We waste all kinds of energy and emotions on negative things.*

Why wasn't he thinking, "I can't wait to meet this guy. I bet we'll be awesome teammates next year."

His time before meeting me would have then been filled with excitement and hope, rather than worry. During that spring, we played little league baseball. My other now business partners, Jason Yates and Beau Cox, played on different teams. However, we developed great relationships that continued throughout the rest of our school years across all sports. The four of us went on to high school and college together before becoming successful business partners.

More Jobs, More Money

I always tend to do things fast. I was always trying to figure out how I could do assignments or tests as efficiently as possible. I wasn't worried about being perfect. I would rather get more done or have more free time. This is something I learned from my dad and my grandfather and something that stayed with me into my business years.

> *The quicker you get a job done, the more jobs you can do, which in turn means more money. That always stuck with me. It was a lesson that time is money.*

Understanding this lesson in business is a must..

This is what separates top producers from average ones. It separates a successful business from those that fail or stay small.

ROCKET FUEL

Figuring out ways to manufacture or buy time is crucial to growth in any company. It starts with personal efficiency and then multiplying yourself and others.

When you hit a ceiling, you expand that ceiling by building another floor, so to speak, or by raising the roof.

Adding people does this, along with building your people.

CHAPTER 15

A New Mentor

"Become Unstoppable and Indestructible"
- Grant Cardone

The Turning Point

Back in 2017, I kept feeling this calling that I needed to be doing more...

I needed to be expanding my reach.

I needed to be inspiring others beyond our company.

I needed to be speaking in front of people.

I needed to be sharing my new perspective on resiliency.

I didn't do anything about it at first. I was comfortable and complacent (my self-proclaimed kryptonite - never a good place to be). My partners and I had a successful mortgage business that we had been running for six years. Money was good, but we were not continuously trying to learn and build, which is imperative in business. We were allowing ourselves to be held over a barrel by many producers who were not team players. We allowed our culture to suffer, which in turn allowed our confidence to slip.

I would come home most nights miserable and would hate to return to the office in the morning.

I was always answering my phone, including when self-centered employees called. This started affecting my family life and the type of dad and husband I was becoming. I'm the type that never runs from problems.

In 2018, something big happened. We had to make a move in our business, and I knew that God was telling me that I needed to make a change in my life. Finally, I remember messaging a friend of mine who I admired as a speaker. Believing he would mentor me, I confided in him about my feelings. He sent me just one sentence. "Grow your following!" I thought, "That's it? That's all you have for me?" I thought he would offer to set up a call with me or something. Still, I accepted his one-line advice. I became obsessed with starting a movement, something people would find attractive. I began waking up every morning and thinking, "How can I do more to get known?" This is something I still do today.

I started reading books and watching online videos to educate myself. I paid a lot of money on courses to hone my speaking and storytelling skills. I booked up to 10 classes a month to practice in front of real estate agents.

I messed up.

I misspoke.

I forgot my material.

But- I kept doing it. I kept booking workshops.

I spoke anywhere I got the chance so I could keep practicing and getting better.

At times I would get frustrated because only a few people would show up or I didn't feel like I did a good enough job.

I kept telling myself, "Keep going! Dad is watching. Can't let him be right."

Then We Lost George...

It was around 1 a.m. on a cold January morning in 2019 when my wife, Jen, woke me up in a panic.

"Your mom just tried to call me. I sent her a text asking if everything was alright and she replied, George died!"

Jen was confused because her phone was on silent and still rang one time and woke her up. She also first thought the text said, "George did" instead of "George died."

You know that feeling when something startles you out of a dead sleep?

That is what we were both dealing with- trying to figure out if we were dreaming or if this was real.

I quickly grabbed my phone and called my mom. She answered frantically . "Oh my God, Mikey, he's dead! What am I going to do? How can I live without him?"

"Breathe," I said.

I was talking to myself as much as I was talking to her.

"Take a deep breath. Are you driving? Where are you? Mom, please, listen to me. I need you to breathe."

I could tell she was driving and I needed to get her calmed down for her own safety. She was hysterical.

I said, "Everything is going to be OK. I need you to be safe right now."

As she took some deep breaths, she let me know she was heading to the hospital. We conferenced my younger brother, Casey, onto the call and he filled me in on what happened.

George went deer hunting that afternoon.

That evening it started to sleet and snow. About an hour after dark, my mom was getting worried because she hadn't heard from George.

At first she thought he must have shot something. After giving enough time for George to have finished with his kill, she called Casey to see if he had heard from George.

Casey and George often went hunting together and kept in close contact when they weren't going together.

Casey and his wife Danielle had two young children, so he wasn't able to go hunting as much as he wanted. Casey said he received a text around 7 p.m. from George saying he was on his way out of the woods. He said he received another text from George saying he was back to his truck safely. At that point, Casey had thought all was good until he got the call from our mom at around 10 p.m.

Casey's heart sunk when he heard from mom. He jumped in his truck and headed straight for the roads where George was hunting. The roads were slippery from the weather.

Casey told me later that he thought George had been involved in an accident.

It was not like George to be unresponsive. He never wanted anyone to worry.

After driving back and forth on the roads from the woods to our parents' home, Casey decided to call the State Police. They informed Casey that George had been taken to the local hospital. Casey called mom and she called the hospital.

The hospital broke the news to her. George didn't make it.

George had had a heart attack as he was pulling out of the parking lot. Instantly he was gone. The truck came to a stop. A guy who lives across the street from where George had parked saw headlights shining towards his house longer than usual. When he went to investigate, he found George.

By the time the EMT arrived, there was nothing they could do.

The whole thing was a huge shock because George was always so healthy. The day before he died, he had just been bragging about hitting 10,000 steps the day before, while he was hunting of course.

Having the three of us on the phone together was much needed. We were able to reassure each other that it was all going to be ok. We would make it through this, and be stronger because of it.

After we hung up, I paced back and forth in my bedroom for hours.

George went the way he always said he wanted to go, while hunting.

It really sucks. We didn't get to say goodbye. I've wished many times for just one more conversation with George.

I felt a sense of guilt laying back down in bed and going to sleep. George had just died and I knew my mom and Casey were in so much pain, but I would need to rest for the days ahead. Our kids were in bed so we would have to break the tough news to them in the morning. Finally I forced myself to lay down and I got a few hours of sleep.

In the morning, my wife and I waited for Nick and Sophie to come downstairs. Nick came down the steps and immediately said, "What's wrong?" He could tell something was not right because Jen and I were never up sitting on the couch in the morning.

Man, what a tough thing to do!

I know people die all the time. Losing a parent is something different than losing anyone else. Breaking the news to the kids was hard.

I remember how hard it was when I learned I had lost my grandparents,. My heart was breaking for our kids.

We sat on the couch, embraced each other, and cried for what felt like hours.

Sophie, six at the time, was next. She loved her Pop-Pop George. She would always imitate his deep voice and mock him for his favorite topics in his deep voice. "Pop-Pop George says, "Hunting for Deers, Cwabs, Fishin', and Baseball!"" George was so passionate about those topics. He was quiet until someone mentioned any of those words.

When Sophie woke up that morning, we broke the news to her.

Surprisingly, she was very matter of fact in her response.

"That's OK. We will see him when we go to Heaven."

> *Wow! Wouldn't it be great for all of us to*
> *be able to handle things like that?*
>
> *There is a lesson there to be learned from a six-year old.*

It blew my mind that she didn't cry or show much emotion. I guess her young brain didn't comprehend the finality of death here on earth.

Lessons From George

My stepdad, George, was both a father and a mentor to me.

Was George hard on me? Yes. Did I get mad at him? Yes. From the time I met George, he drove me hard, as a father should. I would get frustrated when he was hard on me, but when my emotions would calm down, I always understood his message.

> *You see, God knew that as a young boy, I was going to need messages delivered to me in a different way. A hard, direct way.*
>
> *George was that for me. We would talk about whatever it was and I learned from it.*
>
> *One- because I was, and still am, stubborn in my own ways. And two- because I was at a crucial time in my life.*

I needed a father who would stick it out, a father who would not run when things got tough. When George had two children come into his life that he didn't father, he took on that challenge.

Come hell or high water, George was going to see it through, even if he sacrificed everything for it.

Who else do we know from history that was like that?

George once told me that being a stepparent was one of the hardest things he ever had to do. Our mom, at no fault of her own, would often try to soften his discipline while he was guiding and correcting us. He wasn't having any of that.

In those very crucial and impressionable years, going from a boy to a man, you can take one of two roads. Depending on what happens in your life, one of those roads is wider and easier to see and follow.

> *George made my "good road" so much wider and easier to see.*

He didn't have to do that, but that's the kind of man he was. I live every day to make sure his efforts were not in vain and that his spirit, dedication, and dependability live on. He was one of my first true mentors.

After a few months, I started to feel like life was moving on.

It's kind of crazy how life starts to take over again and what happened begins to fade. Of course, it will pop back into your mind from time to time.

I'm not sure if I'm simply accustomed to pushing things to the back of my mind or if I'm being insensitive, but I feel like I have to keep moving. In a sense, I know George would tell me to do that anyway.

I know it shouldn't take him passing to throw gas on my fire, but it did, and the world better look out now.

My Next Mentor

When George passed, I lost my mentor.

Was it now my time to pick up the torch to be that mentor for other people?

I felt ready to be a mentor, but I didn't feel prepared to be my own mentor.

I remembered reading a book back in 2018 called the *10X rule*, written by Grant Cardone. My brother had shared the book with me and said, "Mike you need to read this book, this guy sounds just like you."

While reading that book, I kept feeling that this guy was talking directly to me– isn't that crazy?

I've always had this animal inside me, but it felt like it was caged up and never allowed to be released. I was always scared of what people thought. I was worried I would push people away, or that people would leave my business.

People would tell me you can't be that hard on people, you can't be that direct, people are going to leave us. If you hold people accountable, they won't want to be around you.

Reading the *10X rule* allowed the animal inside of me to come out. I realized I could unleash my superpowers onto the world to accomplish great things and, most importantly, be a role model to help others.

Bottom line, it gave me validation.

When you have validation, you have confirmation, worthiness, and legitimacy.

I needed to not only FEEL unstoppable but to BE unstoppable.

The 10X Rule

On a trip to Miami in February 2019, I noticed billboards advertising the 10X growth conference coming up to be held at the Marlins' stadium. It was being presented as the largest entrepreneur event ever held. To top it off, it was going to compete with the Super Bowl game held on Super Bowl Sunday.

I wanted to go, but I felt I needed to get back home to my family. After I got home, I had a coffee appointment with a real estate agent named Brad. He mentioned he was going to the 10X growth conference in Miami to hear a guy named Grant Cardone.

"You should go."

I am spontaneous and quick to take action, so I immediately bought a $1200 ticket to the conference which was a lot of money for me at the time. Then I went home and told my wife I was going back to Miami to attend a growth conference.

"I need to go; I feel the need to go; I'm going to make it happen."

My wife, Jennifer, has always been very supportive of everything I believe in- that's one of the things that has kept our relationship and marriage so strong for over 17 years. When I decided to go see Grant Cardone, my business partners and I were trying to get our mortgage group off the ground at our new company, Nations Lending. We were one year into our new journey after we had been buried at the previous company. We had big goals that we wanted to reach, but they were nowhere near the ones we would set for ourselves in the months to come.

I was searching for answers, ways to speed up the process and take things to the next level- magic in a bottle.

I found it at the 10X growth conference.

The 10X growth conference is a three-day event. The one I attended was in Miami with over 34,000 people over Super Bowl weekend. There were more than 15 speakers, tons of networking events, and entertainment with hip-hop stars and celebrities.

Grant explained the 10X concept and how it is the one way to guarantee the results you want to have more than you ever thought possible. It really hit me. I thought to myself, "Wow! A guarantee sounds unstoppable to me."

The 10X Rule says:

1) You should set targets for yourself that are 10X greater than what you believe you can achieve.

2) You should take actions that are 10X greater than what you believe are necessary to achieve your goals. The biggest mistake most people make in life is not setting goals high enough.

These two rules are based on the following four mistakes Grant mentions in his book, *The 10X Rule*:

1. Missing targets by setting objectives that are too low and don't allow for enough correct motivation.

2. Severely underestimating what it will take in terms of actions, resources, money, and energy to accomplish the target.

3. Spending too much time competing and not enough time dominating their sector.

4. Underestimating the amount of adversity to overcome to attain a desired goal.

Grant told me I can do way more than I think, and also to just stop thinking and take action. Prior to going to the event, I had been speaking at events in front of real estate agents, teaching them how to market their businesses.

In between the event days, the three people I went to the conference with were riding in the car together discussing the content and the speakers. The guys were telling me I should be up there speaking because they had seen me speak on social media. I thought to myself, "I'm going to be on that stage one day. I know I can do that." I had a clear vision, if they can do it, I know I can do it.

I've always had confidence, stemming from the adversity I've overcome throughout my life.

Your Signature Story

One of the gentlemen speaking on stage at 10X was named Pete Vargas. Pete had a fantastic story about how he started a church youth group. He spoke about his relationship with his father and what it was like to grow up with the conflict.

Even though he was speaking in front of 34,000 people, it felt like I was sitting there in the stadium by myself with Pete speaking directly to me. His story resonated with my relationship with my own biological father.

That was the first time I realized that sharing your story, no matter how ordinary it may seem, does matter.

I was thinking about this as Pete was wrapping up his talk. I found there are three reasons why people don't share their stories.

The first is that people think their story is ordinary and that they need an extraordinary story for people to be interested.

The second is that people may be embarrassed by their story. Maybe they were abused or broken, or had broken people in their family. A lot of people are concerned with how others view them.

The third reason is that people underestimate the power of their story to inspire millions of people.

Pete was offering a workshop on how to develop your story and proprietary process to be able to sell it to help others. I had just won a bunch of money playing in a golf tournament. I thought what a perfect way to take that money and invest in myself. I signed up for the workshop, which was in Aventura Florida, home of Grant Cardone, at his 10X headquarters.

I met some awesome people at the workshop. There were only around 25 people in attendance. I met Pete Vargas, Jarrod Glandt (President of Cardone Enterprises), and Grant Cardone in person. I'm a big believer in developing relationships with people, and there was nothing like getting to meet three of the most impactful people in my life during such a dark time.

What I learned from Pete and Grant during the workshop was crucial in getting my *What Are You Made Of?* podcast started. Get known and connect with your audience by hitting them in the heart.

You see, what drew me to Pete and Grant at the 10X growth conference was how they connected by sharing their story with the audience. It developed a trust that whatever they shared afterwards was believable.

> *This is something I would recommend that you work on- coming up with your signature story, something that happened in your life, as ordinary as it may seem, and sharing it with others. It may feel uncomfortable at first, but you need to lean into it and do it over, and over, and over again. No matter how embarrassing, how ordinary, or how hard it may be to share, this is one of the most powerful connections and relationship building tools that I've ever found.*

What Are Your Intentions?

Now that you have the background, let me share some of the lessons Grant taught me, and some of the things he reminded me of, that will lead you in the right direction to become unstoppable and indestructible.

The first big lesson is about your intentions.

What is it that you intend to do or accomplish?

Where is it that you intend to go or end up?

Who do you intend to go there and do it with?

These are very important questions that you must ask if you want your path to be clear. Without clearly seeing your intentions, you will roam through life, allowing things to happen to you. You will be the effect instead of the cause.

ROCKET FUEL

After going through the things I went through, my intentions at a young age were to make a huge impact on people's lives. I want to be a shining light to people who need it, people who are living in darkness and despair. I saw so much of it as a young child. I was tired of it and didn't want to sit back and allow it to continue without acting. As I got older, I started to realize how big of an impact I could truly have.

The only thing stopping me was… me!

Another important thing. When figuring out your intentions - whatever they are - make them BIG.

Make your intentions so BIG that, when you share them, people think you're crazy.

Why is it so important to go big? Why not strive for just enough to get by?

The reason to go for abundance, beyond having just enough for yourself and your family, is because you need enough to help others, your church, those around you, and generations to come.

Without abundance, it is impossible to be unstoppable and indestructible.

If you had a choice, wouldn't you want to be unstoppable and indestructible?

As Grant helped me realize, I have to be aware of my intentions and my counter intentions. Counter intentions can pull you away from the path to your target. They are the real obstacles of accomplishing your dreams.

For example, if your intention is to be a big Hollywood movie star, but you prefer living in a small town with the friends and family you grew up with, this counter intention to stay might prevent you from achieving your true intention of becoming a big Hollywood movie star.

Or if you want to work on Wall Street, but your counter intention is that you love to live in the suburbs or the country, then this counter intention could prevent you from working on Wall Street.

This lesson is important to become familiar with and to use wisely in auditing what you want and the things that are going to stop you from getting what you want. This allows you to do one of my favorite sayings of all time, "Remove all obstacles!"

Remove All Obstacles

If you want something in life, you need to figure out ways to remove anything that could stop you from it. You need to find ways to go through them, over them, or around them. If you set a goal without this commitment, you will be consistently held up, stopped, set back, and frustrated.

Being aware of this is crucial to becoming unstoppable.

Most people have not clearly identified what they want or where they want to go. Not knowing what could stop you is detrimental to your success. As Lucius Seneca said, "If one does not know to which port one is sailing, no wind is favorable."

One of the biggest challenges people have is that their counter intentions are often intertwined with the people around them regularly, or the people they love, including family and friends.

How are you supposed to handle a family member you love and see regularly when they don't support your dreams?

If they can't think or dream as big as you, maybe they're not supporting you because they can't see your true potential and don't want you to be hurt or disappointed. Is it OK for them to dampen your excitement and enthusiasm for going after your dreams? Of course not!

The last thing I want to do is sound like a preacher to you.

I simply want to share how I've handled it in my life and what has worked for me.

I like to share my dreams and goals with people. It helps me hold myself accountable to those dreams and goals.

I watch for their reaction because it tells me a lot about their thought process and whether or not they will support me.

Take A Mental Note

The first thing I do after noticing their reaction is make a mental note–am I going to hang out with that person more or less? You don't need to make a scene about it, just gradually spend less time with them. You can make some time for them, check in with them, see how they are doing, but, in general, look to spend more time with people that will support you and help you move towards your dreams.

If the people you decide not to hang around with confront you about it, communicate with them your concerns that they are not supportive of your dreams. Let them know how important your dreams and goals are. Let them know you are committed to your goals and you are willing to remove all obstacles to getting them. Welcome those people to be a part of your life if they will be supportive of your goals.

If they are still not supportive after that conversation, it tells you more about them than anything else. From that point on, go hard towards your dreams and goals to make sure you become successful. When you do, the important people meant to be in your life will come back into your life, even if they didn't support you on your journey. You can then decide whether you want them in your life and how much you want them around you.

I know this sounds harsh. I know this is difficult.

It's why most people don't achieve success.

It's too drastic and too difficult of a step for them.

Those that figure this out, and follow through with it, are the ones that excel to extreme levels in all areas of their life.

I've experienced this in my life. When I do this, my circle of people I hang around with shrinks, but it shrinks to the right people.

There can be moments of loneliness and loss when you do this. What keeps me going and getting through those feelings is writing my goals down every single day and remembering why I'm doing what I'm doing.

It's like re-committing every day.

Take Massive Action

The second big lesson I learned from Grant is that, once you've identified your big goals and the obstacles to those goals, you must take massive action. Work towards micro-targets like mile markers leading to your goals. When I was younger, not taking massive action often held me up and kept me from achieving what I wanted to achieve.

When I look back on my past successes, what led up to those successes ALWAYS involved taking massive action.

I've always had the ability to get what I want in life if I set my mind to something AND take massive action.

Grant reminded me that if I want to continue to get what I want out of life, I need to repeat what has worked in the past.

When something works, lean on it, bang on it, do it over and over again. Do whatever it takes. Too many people try to reinvent the wheel because they don't enjoy doing some of the things required to succeed.

It's not about what you like doing or what's fun, it's about what works and gets the job done.

> *Grant Cardone often says, look for what has never let us down and what always works!*

This leads you to accomplishing the most without wasting energy and time. If you are efficient with your time and your energy, when things go wrong you can get back on track faster and blow past your competition.

Quantity Over Quality

As I learned the lesson of massive action, I also learned quantity is greater than quality. If you have high numbers, you can always overcome an error, a bad decision, a bad word, or a moment of weakness.

> *As Grant says, never rely on one of anything.*
> *Not one flow of income, not one person,*
> *not one employee, not one product, not one of anything.*

Confidence And Momentum

I gain a lot of confidence by setting myself up for small victories. No matter what it is, if it's a win and it's taking me towards what I want, I gain confidence from it.

CONFIDENCE

noun

1a: a feeling or consciousness of one's powers or of reliance on one's circumstances had perfect confidence in her ability to succeed met the risk with brash confidence

1b: faith or belief that one will act in a right, proper, or effective way have confidence in a leader

2: the quality or state of being certain : CERTITUDE they had every confidence of success

3a: a relation of trust or intimacy took his friend into his confidence

3b: reliance on another's discretion Their story was told in strictest confidence.

3c: support especially in a legislative body vote of confidence

4: communication made in confidence: SECRET accused him of betraying a confidence

If you are trying to be unstoppable and indestructible, you need success.

If you notice above, in 1a of the definition, it talks about when "the ability to succeed met the risk with brash confidence."

I love the other part as well, "the quality or state of being certain."

When I think of something being unstoppable, I think of the word "certain."

I also think of the word "trust," as mentioned in 3a.

Confidence is like a snowball running down a hill. The more you do to get it rolling, the bigger it becomes, and the greater the momentum.

> *MOMENTUM*
>
> *noun*
>
> *1: a property (see PROPERTY SENSE 1A) of a moving body that the body has by virtue of its mass (see MASS ENTRY 2 SENSE 1C) and motion and that is equal to the product of the body's mass and velocity broadly : a property of a moving body that determines the length of time required to bring it to rest when under the action of a constant force or moment*
>
> *2: strength or force gained by motion or by a series of events. The wagon gained momentum as it rolled down the hill.*

If you notice above in the definition of momentum, the higher your momentum, the longer it takes and the harder it is to stop you. When talking about being unstoppable, this explains why the word momentum must be in the description. Your goal should be to build as much confidence as possible. Higher confidence leads to higher momentum. Never let it slow down.

This works for everything in life, not just business. It also works for your health, your physical shape, your mindset, your relationships, your knowledge, and more.

ROCKET FUEL

Number two in the definition of momentum has a lot to do with being unstoppable and indestructible. The strength and force gained by motion or by a series of events is what I'm talking about.

Getting started is the hardest part.

As you go, momentum builds, which builds speed, which leads to being harder to stop or slow down.

Once you get momentum, everything becomes easier. You need one single ingredient to keep it that way. That one ingredient is activity.

You must keep up the activities that got you where you are.

If you stop, not only will your momentum go away, but your confidence will dwindle. That is where complacency and being comfortable has crept into my life in the past. Analyzing the wins and losses in my past, I've found my momentum dies and my confidence goes away when I get comfortable and complacent.

Success Is Mandatory

The final lesson I want to share with you is that success is our duty and obligation. This is big for Grant, and something I learned from being around him.

Success is not optional, success is non-negotiable.

When you make this mindset shift, the obligation becomes part of your survival- like taking a breath or drinking water.

You can't just say, "I don't feel like taking a breath today."

The same goes for taking action towards a goal.

If you wake up in the morning and don't feel like working out, but you're committed to getting in shape and getting stronger, you just get up and do it anyway.

If you don't feel like making the tough phone calls you need to make, just do it anyway.

If you're uncomfortable with anything you need to do towards an action to get you to accomplish your dreams, just do it anyway.

Success is a muscle that you build. The more you do it, the easier it is to overcome the negative voice in your head and the negative feelings that try to keep you from taking the actions necessary to achieve your goals.

These lessons, as simple as they may sound, are the fundamentals to achieving anything you set your mind to do. I hope you take the time to implement these in your life so that you too can be unstoppable and indestructible.

Stop being satisfied with mediocre.

CHAPTER 14

What Are You Made Of?

"Spend a lifetime learning."
- Richard Dolan

Don't Be A Hard Head!

"The minute you're not learning, I believe you're dead."
- Jack Nicholson

Now that you know where I'm coming from and where I'm heading, please open your mind and be willing to learn. Always be a sponge for information. You can do it. One of the worst things you can do is think that you know it all and that you cannot be shown or taught new things and new ideas.

Learn, Learn, Learn

Being stuck in your ways can be detrimental to your success, growth, and survival. If you're in a rut, the quickest way out is to learn something new. Watch a video, listen to a podcast, or even better, read a book like you're doing now.

ROCKET FUEL

A big problem in our country, and the world, is that people refuse to learn new things. When this happens, you see prejudice, racism, and beliefs that limit people from accomplishing great things.

One who continuously learns can assist his own life, and the lives of everyone around them. Refusing to learn puts you in a selfish, imperious state.

There is no advancement in life when people stop learning.

This is why I've dedicated a whole chapter to learning. Most of the things we currently believe, true or not, come from other people.

Some things have been beaten into our heads so much that we don't even know if they're true.

I remember my stepfather, George, always telling me when I was a teenager that I needed to read more. He would tell me that reading increases intelligence, which increases understanding of life, and ability to communicate with people. For some reason, I couldn't wrap my head around what he was trying to tell me at that age. I relied on hustle, common sense, and street smarts.

At one point in my life, I realized that no matter how hard I worked or how much action I took, I could not advance to where I wanted to advance.

I was missing something.

So, I started searching online to find others who were in that same predicament. I searched for people who had gotten to a point where they felt like they had hit a ceiling and couldn't go any further, and then had found a way to go higher.

The common thing I kept hearing from those that had made it through to the next level was that the answers were found in books and mentors. The difference maker is knowledge. When you don't know something, it impedes progress.

It wasn't until I was in my late 30s that I started to gain real book smarts.

I became an obsessed maniac with learning. Every time I was in an airport, I would buy one or two new books. I started carrying a backpack while traveling just to carry my books to read in the airport and on the plane.

I try to be as open-minded as possible when I read. I try to think about times in my past where the concepts I was reading were applied, without me really being conscious of it.

I also look for new concepts I haven't heard before. I think what might have happened if I had applied those in the past, and where I would be with my business and my life.

I also watch YouTube videos from people who are in places I want to be in, or are on a journey to where I want to go..

Podcasts are another thing I've found helpful in learning.

I use all of these things in combination with each other, to absorb as much information as possible. I take notes in a journal about the things I'm learning.

Then I started posting on social media about what I was learning. I would quote others, giving them credit while I was sharing the information with my followers online.

I am the type of person that likes to share things that work for me with other people. I think it had to do with growing up around so many broken people. I was always trying to help people.

I became almost an evangelist of self-improvement and business strategies.

However, I reached a point where I felt I needed to start creating my own content. I don't think there is anything new as far as concepts, but I do believe there are different points of view and other ways to frame concepts so more people understand them. I recommend taking this action like I did, as early as possible in your life. No matter where you are, young or old.

One trick that works for me to get through books without getting bored or getting overwhelmed with the information, is to read ten pages in the morning and ten pages at night. If I do this with a 30-day month, I read 600 pages a month, representing two to three books. The average person reads one book a year!

I'm able to absorb and read around 30 books a year.

Can you imagine the information available from 30 books?

If you want to be unstoppable and indestructible, get obsessed with learning.

I was one of the most hard-headed and stubborn people you could meet. If I can realize how important it is to continue to gain knowledge, than you can too.

ROCKET FUEL

I have now focused that stubbornness into being committed and determined to learn and soak up as much knowledge as possible.

Reading Is Learning

If my goal is to help you launch into the life of your dreams, we have to start with the fundamentals, the foundation. Before we can fill with ROCKET FUEL, we must first make sure we are competent enough to use it.

I often stopped reading books halfway through, and even stopped reading altogether. I had a lot of half-read books lying around. I didn't feel good about myself for not finishing the books. The fact is, I could have finished a book, but there was something holding me back.

It was more than just being stubborn and thinking I knew everything. The biggest thing causing me not to want to learn or read was my lack of comprehension of certain words in the books I was reading. I would stop reading a book when I came to a topic or word I didn't understand. Instead of looking up the definition, I would get frustrated, lose interest, and quit. Doing this doesn't get you excited about picking up another book to read.

When my stepdad, George, used a word I didn't understand, he wouldn't tell me what it meant. He would tell me to get a dictionary. We didn't have "Google." My dictionary was an actual book with words and definitions in it. I always wondered why he wouldn't just tell me what the word meant. George was smart but I was too stubborn and hard-headed to pick up on what he was trying to tell me. It was only after he had passed, and I had gone on this knowledge-seeking journey, that I understood why he told me to look up words in a dictionary.

When I started looking up definitions of words, it changed everything for me. I felt like I could learn anything, or read any book and comprehend what was in it. It gave me that unstoppable feeling. This is one of the biggest pieces of the formula to becoming unstoppable.

Have you heard the phrase Knowledge is Power?

I experienced this and have added it to my ROCKET FUEL formula.

Comprehension is essential in the process of learning.

LEARN

verb

1a: gain or acquire knowledge of or skill in (something) by study, experience, or being taught.

1b:become aware of (something) by information or from observation.

2a: commit to memory, memorize

2b: to come to be able

2c: to come to realize

COMPREHEND

verb

1: to grasp the nature, significance, or meaning of

These two things allow you to become more competent and more confident in the areas of your life in which you are gaining knowledge. Sorting out the false from the true creates an opportunity like coming out of the woods and seeing a whole new world view.

There are a lot of issues socially and personally that arise when people refuse to learn. This goes for leaders of businesses, communities, and nations.

Most conflicts between countries, and within countries, have stemmed from the leadership of those countries stuck in their ways. Either from false information or because they refuse to learn anything new. We can see huge differences for a country when a single leader commits to learning, so imagine the power of learning when a large number of individuals commit to learning.

ROCKET FUEL

One of my mentors, Richard Dolan, the performance coach for the Los Angeles Lakers, LeBron James, Miami Heat, and many more, told me:

> *"When you block something, you fight it. When you fight something, you resist it. When you resist something, it persists."*

This can pertain to many things, like something you need to do, a conversation you need to have, or something you need to learn and comprehend. Resisting to learn and comprehend something causes your lack of knowledge to persist. This leads to insecurities that are unnecessary.

If people would understand this, the world would be a better place.

Think of all the social issues that could be healed by people gaining more knowledge and having fewer insecurities and anxieties.

From The Source

Before accepting information as knowledge, always consider your source.

Make sure what you are learning is coming from an expert, someone with credibility who has studied, experienced, and accomplished what they are teaching.

Do not be fooled into taking guidance from someone who claims to be a "teacher" or "coach" without any personal experience.

The information you receive will be questionable, to say the least.

Remember, we are seeking the truth here. The last thing you want to do is spend time learning false information and creating belief systems around those false beliefs.

The way I approach this on my journey of gaining knowledge is to seek out mentors. The best way to find the right mentor is to first get clear on what it is you want and where you want to go. Then search out someone who has done what you want to do or is where you want to be.

Mentoring doesn't have to be done in person.

Most of the possible mentors that you are going to run into are not that accessible.

Do some research and see if your potential mentors have published any content in print or online. See if they have any events you can attend. If you don't have money to invest at this time, look for free info that mentors push out on free platforms.

Immerse Yourself

One of the best ways to learn a new language is to immerse yourself in the language. It's the same with learning from a mentor. The more time you spend around them or their content, the more it helps speed up the process.

Once you've learned about them, reach out to them and find out how you can add value to them. Maybe it's purchasing a program from them, buying a book, or going to one of their events.

This is what I do.

I want to learn everything I possibly can and know the blueprint my mentors use to get where they are. This speeds up the process and helps me detour the mistakes my mentors made in their journeys. I make sure to surround myself with people who consistently think the same way.

Some people think I'm crazy and obsessed, but those that have been on this journey understand the end game. You're either moving forward and achieving higher levels or you're falling backward.

This explains why, all of a sudden, people are reaching out to me to assist them with issues they have. They are now interested in what I'm accomplishing and asking me questions about how I got here.

The Hater Cycle

There's a cycle I call the "hater cycle." I love watching the hater cycle. When you make changes in your life to better yourself, some people around you will get uncomfortable because you are changing. They feel a need to justify in their minds why they are not making progress forward. They'll question you, ridicule you, and make fun of you to make themselves feel better.

ROCKET FUEL

Suppose you don't let their behavior stop you, but instead convert that negative energy into ROCKET FUEL to use for your mission. When you do, you'll notice people start getting interested in what you're doing. They may still throw a few jabs, but it will be less jabbing and more watching.

If you keep going and don't quit, those same people will start to admire you. They will begin to ask you questions and then even start rooting for you. You may even hear them saying they knew you were going to be a success all along.

This is the hater cycle. If you know it ahead of time, you can enjoy watching it happen.

How Many Mentors?

I often get asked how many mentors is the right number. The "more the merrier" is not always the case. I've noticed many of the same people in the groups I hang in talking about multiple mentors they are involved with.

These people do not seem to accomplish a lot, but they are always in the groups. They are soaking up knowledge with very little follow-up action.

What I see happening here is they are listening to too many people and getting conflicting information. This tends to happen when you have too many mentors.

When you have conflicting information and try to act, you get paralyzed because you do not have a true direction.

And Change

Do an inventory of the people around you. Make a note of the ones who are supporting and encouraging you and pushing you to higher levels.

Also note the ones who are holding you back and discouraging you.

You hear a lot of people say, "Get rid of people in your life if they're not lifting you up."

However, I think blocking people from your life reduces your ability to inspire people. I recommend limiting your time around people who are holding you back, but not eliminating them. It helps to understand that what they say tells you more about them than it does about you. Take it with a grain of salt.

Also, take note of the activities you are regularly doing. Eliminate those that are not taking you towards your goals.

What words are you saying consistently that are keeping you back?

What thoughts are you repeating in your mind that you need to eliminate?

To gain knowledge, you need to make room for it.

What is it that you're going to get rid of?

To change, you must give something up.

ROCKET FUEL

CHAPTER 13

Get Clarity

"You Need Clear Skies to Launch for The Stars."
- Jarrod Glandt

Think Big

Everything in life changed for me when I started thinking big. When I say big, I'm talking so big that when you tell your family and friends about it, they look at you like you're crazy. They start saying things like, "Yeah right" and "Aren't you happy where you are?" They start giving you reasons why you can't do it.

They may even laugh at you and make jokes.

These unsupportive actions don't necessarily make you want to quit on your big goals and dreams right away. They gnaw at you and build up to the point where you eventually quit.

If you're thinking big enough, you get scared. You start having voices in your head asking you if you really want to do it. You start running into days where you feel like quitting because it seems too hard. You even start to think you're crazy. However, going for big also makes you excited. It makes you want to do whatever it takes. If you don't feel excited by your goals, and you don't feel like you would do whatever it takes to get them, then they're not big enough.

People that tell you to set realistic goals have a limiting belief problem.

None of us know our full potential. How could we ever come to realize our full potential by setting "realistic goals?" Anything that is realistic sounds boring to me and makes me want to fall asleep. These kinds of low-level goals will not give you the thrust needed to launch into the life of your dreams.

Get Excited

When you start setting BIG goals that make you excited and scared at the same time, your friends, co-workers, and your spouse may get sick of hearing about them.

When you're thinking big enough, you get obsessed and talk about it all the time. When you talk about it all the time, some people might feel insecure with the fact that they don't think as big as you. Instead of encouraging you, they tend to get annoyed. They redirect their negative feelings towards you.

This happened to me. When I decided to get known globally, to be the guy who teaches people how to turn setbacks, difficulties, letdowns, and negativity into ROCKET FUEL for their future, along with starting the *What Are You Made Of?* podcast, I heard it from everyone.

If I had let even one person stop me, let alone all the people who cracked jokes, questioned my decisions, and doubted me, I would not be where I am today.

I belong to a golf club in Maryland. I had a conversation with one of my buddies from the club. He was bothered by some of the group comments he had heard directed at my mission. I told my friend that this is part of the process and how it says more about them than it does about my mission.

He then asked me to tone it down a little bit because I was bothering some people at the club. I told him that if there was a problem, they could suck it up and deal with it, or I didn't need to be a member of the club. My mission is bigger than my membership at a golf club.

What's funny about the whole thing is that I am doing all of this to help other people and to make those supporting me proud.

In our mortgage group, we set out a goal to do 20 times more in production than what we were currently doing. I had to first convince my leadership team to start thinking bigger. Then I had to get our team of 20 employees on board. When we shared our massive goals, some of the people at corporate would chuckle.

When we would have a month where we doubled our production, I would tell leadership we were just getting started and we don't want to celebrate yet. They would say, "You're doing great. You should be happy where you are."

I would share their comments with the team as ROCKET FUEL for them and push themselves further and harder.

If you want to accomplish big things, you need to elevate. As you hit micro-targets on the way to your goals, and when you hit your goals, you must always elevate them to the next level. If you stop and settle for where you are, you will never know where your potential lies.

As long as we are alive on this planet, we must have a challenge or a problem to solve. If we do not, we begin dying.

It is important to note that ultimately a decision has to be made. Are you going to go for your dreams, or are you going to stay around those who are doubting you, are unsupportive, and have quit on their own lives and dreams?

This decision for me was difficult. I wasn't even aware that I had given up on my dreams. Subconsciously, you may find yourself going along with the crowd because your brain tells you this is what you need for security and survival.

Our brain is designed to encourage us to be in a herd. It is safer to be in a herd than it is to be alone because of predators. But, a herd doesn't help you if they are discouraging you, degrading you, laughing at you, criticizing you, or generally not being supportive. Find a herd that is pushing you, cheering you, lifting you up, and helping you achieve your goals.

More on this in a later chapter.

I want to put into context how BIG I'm talking when it comes to goals.

I'm also going to cover things that will come up when you try to set big goals so you can be aware of them and understand that they're normal. Then we'll talk about how to handle them.

ROCKET FUEL

Why Rocket Fuel?

How does all of this relate to ROCKET FUEL?

We are learning to fill our tanks with ROCKET FUEL, but without goals we have no direction. The goal is to give us a destination to head towards with the ROCKET FUEL we put in our tanks.

But why such big goals? Remember, the larger the goal, the more abundant the thinking.

Abundance creates growth, scarcity leads to death.

95% of people never make it anywhere because of the limitations in our own minds. Most of us have been programmed from a young age to believe that our limits are well below our true potential.

Nothing Is Impossible

"The day before something is truly a breakthrough, it's a crazy idea."

- Peter Diamandis.

If something seems impossible, it's just because it hasn't been done yet.

There are things happening today that would have seemed impossible five years ago. We use products as commonplace today that would have seemed science fiction even five to ten years ago.

A mobile phone with the capabilities of face-to-face video call was something that, as a kid, I used to watch on cartoons. Video meetings on your laptop with people on the other side of the world seemed an impossibility to me as a kid.

Anything that stops you from thinking big, or makes things appear impossible to you, needs to be converted in your mind to ROCKET FUEL for your mission.

Setting any goal, no matter how big or small, takes energy and effort.

Goals, both big and small, will come with setbacks, letdowns and negative people.

So, if you're going to do it, why not do it BIG?

Visualization And Clarity

To avoid limiting myself, I often imagine I have a magic lamp with a genie inside. The genie grants me five to ten wishes - screw only getting three wishes. Who wants only three?

I clearly and specifically visualize having everything I want. I write it down with pen and paper in a notebook.

There is something magical about putting pen to paper.

Do not type it into your phone or computer. Although typing it is better than not doing it at all, studies have shown that your brain reacts differently when writing rather than typing.

- What is my purpose or mission?
- How much money do I want to earn?
- Where is it that I want to be?
- What kind of spouse and family do I want?
- What kind of spouse and parent do I want to be?
- Who do I want to be around?
- What kind of person do I want to be?
- How do I want to impact others?
- What kind of shape do I want for myself?
- How do I want to feel?
- Who do I want to help?
- How many people do I want to help?

Be Clear And Specific

When I write my visualizations down, I do so as if they are already happening.

I try to train my brain into making these a reality.

You may have heard people telling you to write down your goals annually, quarterly, or monthly. My mentor, Grant Cardone, preaches to do it three times a day - when you first wake up in the morning, right before you go to bed, and anytime you have a setback or are doubting that you're on the right track.

Writing your goals down three times a day may sound obsessive and ridiculous, but we want ridiculous results. I feel I need to sell myself repeatedly on why I do what I do. I write down my goals three times a day. It works for me

Life Is Hard

No matter how good you are, or how good your intentions are, bad things will still happen to you.

Writing your goals down three times a day gives you ROCKET FUEL to push through the bad things and towards your target.

It recommits you.

Why Not?

Why don't people use the powerful technique of setting goals and visualizing them? There are several reasons. Most people struggle in at least one of these areas:

1. They might not know about it.

2. It takes time and effort, and people don't want to sacrifice those things when they don't know the benefits.

3. They operate with a set of programmed, limiting beliefs.

4. It takes commitment, discipline, and patience.

Make It Happen

Here are four benefits of clear visualization and writing your goals down three times a day:

1. It creates clear intentions, prepares you, and gives you a destination each day to move towards. Success follows preparation. A destination

allows you to set up a direction for you to move. By doing this, you are operating with intentionality. You are in proactive mode rather than reactive mode. This puts YOU in control.

2. By visualizing your goals ahead of time, you train your brain to believe you've already accomplished what you're writing down. You now BELIEVE IT'S POSSIBLE TO DO because, in your mind, YOU'VE ALREADY DONE IT.

3. It lowers anxiety and stress. Did you know that most anxiety and stress come from people feeling they should be accomplishing more but are not? Visualizing creates clarity in your mind.

4. When you go big, you stretch and reach for your potential. It is the only way to find out what you are made of.

It Works

It really isn't rocket science, it's just ROCKET FUEL. And it works.

All you need to do is commit to doing it.

Put your foot down. Be done with living a reactionary life. Be done with a mediocre and anxious way of living. Every thought we have, every word we speak, and every action we take leads us towards our goals or away from them. There is no inbetween. Visualizing clearly and then writing down your goals three times a day helps you decide what to think, say, and do.

> *I'm bringing this to you from my experience and the success I've seen it bring into my life and into the lives of others.*

Here's to clear skies and a successful launch of your life amongst the stars!

CHAPTER 12

Culture is the Foundation of Success

*"Culture isn't just one aspect of the game, it is the game.
In the end, an organization is nothing more than
the collective capacity of its people to create value."*
- Lou Gerstner

The Culture Awards Ceremony

Culture is so important in business, in family, and in any relationship you have. If you don't have the right culture, that relationship or business likely won't be around long.

In a previous life- a previous mortgage company- the office was like a Wall Street boiler room. There were close to twenty of us on the phones, making sales calls all day, trying to make money by helping people refinance to save money.

We would have great months, huge months.

We were making money by helping people out.

We didn't have the perfect culture, but it was a good culture, good enough for us to work and be successful.

We had awards and ceremonies to celebrate big sales and big months. We had awards for Loan Officer of the month and big lotto checks. It was a little corny, but it really mattered to us. We fed off of it. Everyone was vying for the number one spot. We had a lot of fun and a lot of success.

The Crisis Hit

The 2008 housing crisis and mortgage crash really impacted our business. We all felt it.

Big changes happened in the industry. Everybody had to get licensed through a standardized licensing process. Many people in our group, and many around the industry, fell out of the business because they couldn't pass the test or didn't want to try.

We went from almost twenty people to less than five. It was that big of a drop-off. Many people got out of the business and many others stayed and struggled to find their way. A lot of my friends lost their jobs and their livelihoods. Our culture died.

Let's Go!

Incomes were a lot less. We stopped tracking numbers. There were no more big checks, no more awards. We started living in scarcity, just trying to survive. None of us wanted to be in a different profession.

One day I went to my friend, and now business partner, Chris Short, and suggested we open our own branch. I said, "Let's go out on our own. We've got to do something. We can't just sit here. We can't continue doing what we're doing right now. It's not working."

He came back after talking to his wife and said, "I'm ready to move. Talked to my wife. Let's hit the road. Let's go for it." His wife was ready to pack up, move, and sell their house.

Without hesitation I said, "All right, let's do this. It isn't going to be easy. We need to commit at this moment that we aren't going to let anything stop us. When we hit obstacles and tough spots, we are either going to go through them, around them, or over them."

I didn't waste time once he agreed. I didn't want to give him a chance to change his mind. I was ready to go full force, full steam ahead.

We had no idea how we would do it.

We just had it in our heads that we were going to make things happen, and that we would be able to figure it out as we went along.

We wanted to move towards the beach in Ocean City, Maryland. It was a more laid-back area than where we were in Annapolis.

We had no mentors at the time. If I could go back and give myself advice, it would be to find a mentor. I can't overstate the value of mentors in helping accomplish your goals.

Have Faith

The owner of the company told us we were going to fail. His lack of faith made me feel just like I'd felt when my biological father crumpled up that hundred dollar bill and threw it at me, telling me I was going to be living on the streets with my mom one day.

That stubborn little C-Roc came out and said, "We'll show you!"

I turned the owner's belief that we would fail into ROCKET FUEL to succeed.

Commit

It was 2011. We put our family's finances and the whole thing on the line.

We put it up and we committed.

We rented an office space in Salisbury, Maryland from my old buddy, Joe. I had worked for Joe at his water treatment company years earlier.

We put two desks in this little office and started our business, grinding and really going for it.

There were a lot of sleepless nights, and a lot of stress.

The Right People

We knew we couldn't do it ourselves. If we wanted to grow and scale, we had to have people. We also knew we needed the right culture. We started searching for the right people, one person at a time.

We found a lady named Beverly who had never been in the mortgage business. I liked the idea of hiring someone with no experience in the mortgage business. We could train them from the ground up and groom them into our culture of what we were looking to do. I just needed someone willing to work hard, buy in, and have a dream.

Beverly was the first employee to start with us and she's still with us today.

We gradually added one, added one, added one.

In eight years we've rarely lost an employee that we didn't want to lose.

The employees that are still with us are the ones we've wanted.

We learned important lessons between 2011 and today that I want to share with you.

Culture Is Everything

We knew we needed a good culture, but we really didn't know what this meant when we started. We didn't understand everything that goes into it. We are still learning today, but there are some big things we've implemented that have turned our group into an attraction model.

You can apply these in your business, family, and relationships.

If you're an employee, you can make your workplace a better place for other people around you. You can also work with your family and develop a better culture. No matter how good you get at this, there's always room for growth.

At our previous company, there were people who didn't have the culture in mind and didn't care about the team. They were 'me-people,' worried only about themselves. "What's in it for me?"

They wanted to keep all the money and didn't want the company, owner, or managers to make any of it.

It was all about them instead of about the team. They missed the important point that, without an owner, there is no company and, without a company, they have no place to work.

We failed to develop the right culture because we didn't put our foot down. We needed to lay the groundwork with realistic expectations and accountability, and stay committed to it.

"You're either going to do this, or you're not going to work here anymore."

It must be done this way. It won't work otherwise.

You might have some short-term success, but long-term success requires a good culture.

Without a good culture, at some point it will come crumbling down. Those that are not held accountable and that don't buy into the culture will only look out for themselves. They will make decisions that will benefit them without thinking about how it might hurt the team. This will crush your culture and your team/company/family.

Great Foundation, Great People

"A company's culture is the foundation for future innovation.
An entrepreneurs job is to build the foundation." - Brian Chesky

In February 2018 we made the switch to partner with Nations Lending. We understood we needed to lay the right groundwork and foundation from the start. We weren't going to work with producers that didn't care about the team. We decided that team players and culture fit were more important attributes than being a top producer. We hired first for culture and mindset, even if the people we hired still needed to work on themselves and their professional abilities.

This is the route we went. We put the right building blocks in place so that, as we got to the tough times that always come up as you build a business, we could get through them with our great foundation and our great people.

We all understood what we were trying to accomplish. We had shared goals, a common target, and a big vision. We were all on the same page.

Acceptance, Mediocrity, Average

You have to constantly be working on culture and buy in. It took a good six to eight months to get everybody brought in at Nations Lending. We focus daily on culture. It's important to watch and hold each other accountable.

We call each other out when we are falling off track because one little slip-up, or one little thing that slides, becomes contagious, like a virus throughout your organization.

We must be very, very conscious of it.

You must be highly sensitive to anything that can affect culture in a negative way. The problem many companies run into is that they let small things slide. When something that should be done daily gets missed one day without being corrected, it establishes a routine and trains people in the wrong way.

"Hey, that's okay. One time, that's okay."

Then it happens again.

"Hey, it happened last time. It's okay. Nothing big will really happen from that."

You quickly start to have a culture of acceptance, of mediocrity, and the average. It starts chipping away at what you need to be successful. You can't let that happen. You must recognize it as soon as possible and call it out.

"Tolerating a problem has the same consequences as failing to identify it. Once you identify a problem, don't tolerate it." - Ray Dalio

Sometimes, I feel like a jerk when I do this, but I recognize the positive results that come from doing it. When you start holding people accountable for a culture, one of two things is going to happen.

Either people will turn and run, leaving your organization, or they're going to step it up and strive for greatness. If they leave, they aren't a good fit for the culture. If they stay, they are primed for you to bring greatness out of them.

Those are the two things that can happen.

Once you understand that these are the two outcomes, you no longer worry about being a jerk, because you are only being a jerk to those who don't fit the culture.

Run Or Push Forward

It's all about the team, the vision, and the culture. You either want people to run from it or lean into it.

There is no middle ground. If you push people and they leave, you are in a better place because they were not going to conform to the culture. They were not going to do what was needed to succeed and for the company to be successful.

This is important to remember.

Nobody's perfect.

We're all human. Days go differently than expected, we get caught up in things, bad things happen to good people. At the end of the day, you need to have a little voice that says to you, "Hey, I've got to get back on track."

It's okay to have a bad day here and there. Don't beat yourself up over them.

You're going to have bad days. You just gotta get back on track.

You need to have people holding you accountable.

This Is What I Do Everyday

I'm in the people building business. It just happens that mortgages are our vehicle.

I strive to build people, get greatness out of them, and help them work towards their goals and visions.

This is what it's all about for me.

My passion for building people is what gets me out of bed in the morning.

ROCKET FUEL

I try to build my co-workers, my friends, and my family. Although my family can be a bit more difficult to coach. I think my kids got the stubbornness gene from me.

Create A Great Culture

My team and I developed Four Pillars of Culture. We developed these pillars for our business, but they also work for family, friends, and with any group or community.

FIRST PILLAR: GRATITUDE

Gratitude is the key to happiness. When gratitude is practiced regularly and from the heart, it leads to a richer, fuller and more complete life.
-Vishen Lakhiani

Develop a mindset of gratitude. You must have gratitude among your group.

Emails, phone calls, and handwritten cards are all meaningful, but you also need to set aside time to publicly show gratitude to each other. I'm talking about in a meeting or on a stage, either a physical stage or virtual stage like a company intranet or a team app like Slack.

You need to show gratitude to people. Let them know you appreciate them. Not just by saying it, but by showing them. Be specific with your gratitude. Being specific shows you are being genuine and sincere.

Let people know you are noticing their efforts when they go above and beyond. One thing we do in our organization is to start our weekly sales meeting with a gratitude period. It has worked well for us and I recommend you consider doing something similar. In the gratitude period, we go around the room and each person names someone on the team and thanks them for something they did the week before that went above and beyond. Nobody can repeat the same thing.

It will take time from the rest of the meeting, it will take time from the day, but the benefits from the time it takes will be well worth it. It's the right thing to do and it makes people feel good. Gratitude has changed the ballgame for us.

We hear our processors thanking our loan officers, our managers thanking our processors, and everyone recognizing the hard work that others are doing. It's nice to be recognized. It alleviates stress and helps people feel valued for their efforts.

SECOND PILLAR: VISION AND ALIGNMENT

When you develop a culture in a company, a family, or any group, you need to have a clear group vision and specific group targets and goals. These give everyone a common direction and destination.

Set big, unreasonable group goals.

The word "reasonable" has a meaning that is limited. Our minds, and society, set self-imposed limits when we think in terms of what's "reasonable."

We don't want to be reasonable, we want to be unreasonable. We're not able to comprehend what we're truly capable of, it simply isn't possible. So set unreasonable, massive targets and goals that push beyond the limitations of your beliefs. Targets and goals that are "unreasonable."

When you set unreasonable goals, it forces the limits, the ceiling in your brain, to rise and push past what you thought possible.

It works.

You should feel disappointed if you blow away a goal. It means you set a goal that was realistic and way too low. It means you left something on the table.

> *You should have set a higher goal because you could have attained and accomplished so much more.*

No individual will buy into a group's mission without feeling the group, and the leader of the group, genuinely cares about their individual goals and needs. This is where a lot of leaders mess up. They are consumed with what they want and where they want the company to go. They neglect the individual's personal, professional, and financial goals.

Here is where ROCKET FUEL is added to a group's mission. When you get people on board with a mission by aligning the group's goals with the individual's goals, you become unstoppable. A leader needs to find out her team members' goals and make sure those goals align with the team's goals. If this step is missed, conflict arises. It's like a salmon swimming upstream, not allowing the stream to flow properly. Business is hard enough without adding extra conflict, especially when it's unneeded and easily avoided.

The other reason for finding out what your team members' goals are is to have something as a benchmark for growth and hold them accountable. You can't hold someone accountable without their permission and without knowing how to hold them accountable. This one step will change your business. You get what you measure.

THIRD PILLAR: UNLIMITED INCOME POTENTIAL

Some people don't understand money. They live paycheck to paycheck. They're in debt and feel trapped in a job where they can't go anywhere.

We wanted to establish a place where people didn't feel trapped or like they were unable to obtain their financial goals. We wanted to break this limiting beliefs. We established unlimited income potential for all our employees. We took the limits off income. All our loan officers can produce as much as they want. They can make as much money as they want.

Still, our support staff were limited. They had to rely only on the loan officers to bring in the loans. So we created a system to pay for the support staff to get licensed if they want to become producers. This allows them to generate leads as simply as ending calls with, "Hey, by the way, who do you know that could use some honest help with a mortgage?" Or "Who do you know that is buying or selling in the next six months?" All they have to do is end the conversation with a short question and it can create income for them.

By providing this path, we now have a system where anyone can make as much money as they want, an unlimited amount.

We don't stop there. If any employee ever wants to move up in the organization, all they need to do is tell us in our goal meetings. We then set up a roadmap for them to accomplish their goal.

> *You must allow people to grow in business and relationships.*

If you think about a flower in a pot, at some point that flower is going to break the pot or stop growing and die. You need to be willing to move it to a bigger pot so that it can continue its growth. This is how we think. We grow people. We have to provide an environment and a culture for them to do that.

Every person in our organization can move up and have unlimited income potential.

> *We have a culture where everybody is lifting each other up, cheering for each other, and celebrating each other's wins. It needs to be constantly maintained, but it works and it's worth it.*

FOURTH PILLAR: ACCOUNTABILITY

The final pillar is accountability. There must be systems in place to hold people accountable. Accountability helps everyone stay on track and helps get us back on track when we slip. Our systems have people holding other people accountable.

Sometimes it takes a little bit of a "Hey, let's go! Get it together." You don't always have to be so nice with it because some people need that extra push.

We set stretch goals that push people out of their comfort zone. We don't grow in our comfort zones. It's good to get that little tough love in there sometimes when people aren't pushing to their potential.

Leadership and accountability are the responsibility of every team member and are imperative attributes for living the life of your dreams. We will talk more about them in a later chapter.

ROCKET FUEL

We are guided by our mission and our goals and what we are trying to accomplish. Everyone understands why we are doing the things we're doing. If someone on the team isn't doing what they're supposed to do, it affects everyone. It's our duty and obligation to call each other out when we're off track - respectfully of course. We are family and it's part of our culture to call each other out and to not get defensive when someone calls us out.

CHAPTER 11

The Blueprint for Indestructible Relationships

"Communication is Everything"
- Jen Ciorrocco

Help

I'm writing this book because I want to help people. I needed help in my life and I want to be that for you. I want to make a difference in the world. I'm very thankful to have you as a reader. This chapter is about how to convert setbacks, let-downs, and bad times in your relationships into ROCKET FUEL to thrust your relationship to the next level.

Greater and Greater Relationships

We all hope our relationships will get better day by day, week after week, year after year.

Unfortunately many relationships don't follow that curve.

Why?

ROCKET FUEL

Why do so many relationships go downhill?

Shouldn't relationships start great and then get even better?

It seems that not enough emphasis is put on developing and building strong relationships.

How do you make relationships indestructible? Not just relationships with your partner, but all your relationships at home, at work, with friends, and in the community.

Be Intentional

You have to be intentional in your relationships.

People in healthy relationships improve over time.

It's the unhealthy relationships that start great and then go downhill.

Relationships become unhealthy when you stop being intentional.

Being intentional in your relationships means you are always working to improve them.

A Two-Way Street

Never forget, a relationship is a two-way street.

A relationship is not meant to serve one person. A relationship is meant to serve each other.

When two people work together to serve and support each other for a greater purpose, that's a great place to start building a relationship.

> *Nobody's perfect. The goal isn't to be perfect. The goal is to continue to push to be the best you can. The best spouse, the best friend, parent, employer, employee. I want to be the best I can. The fact that you're reading this book suggests you want the same.*

Growing Apart Or Growing Together?

People change. People grow.

Are your relationships growing together or apart? We often hear people in failed relationships say, "We grew apart."

If you're not growing, you're dying, but when you're growing, you're changing. It's important to be sharing those changes with the people you want to stay close to. If you want to grow together instead of apart, you need to have common goals and understand each other's growth.

Communication, More Than Words

Communication is key to any healthy relationship.

When relationships start to lack communication, couples often live separate lives even when they are still in a relationship. They treat each other like roommates instead of partners.

They sleep in the same bed together, but they are worlds apart.

> *Communication is not just words.*
>
> *It's a touch, it's an attitude.*
>
> *It's verbal and it's non-verbal.*

Often relationships feel perfect at the start. There's even a term for it, the honeymoon phase.

Everything is great, then you start to realize the other person isn't perfect. You start holding them to a higher standard, sometimes an unreasonable standard.

You can't expect anyone to be perfect. Remember, when you point the finger, it's often more a reflection of yourself than it is of the other person.

Compliment Your Partner

Life brings a lot of pressures. There are pressures at work and at home. Being in a relationship can also generate a lot of pressure, especially when kids and other factors are involved. Sometimes the pressure gets hard to turn off.

Be considerate of the other person and compassionate for what they're going through. Acknowledge that they are going through things in their life that you don't understand and things you don't even know about.

Don't get caught in the bullying game of saying, "You should be doing this better," or "This should be what your focus is."

The kind of questions you should be asking are questions like, "What can I do to make my partner feel good today?" and "What can I do to be a hero to my partner?"

Show compassion.

Seek to understand things from their perspective.

Let go of your ego.

Anytime you see an opportunity to lift your partner up, do it.

Celebrate wins with each other.

Tell the other person how proud you are of them for accomplishing something.

It's Not 50/50, It's 100/100

It's easy to be stuck within ourselves and only think about our own feelings and our own perceptions.

In a relationship, people say everything is 50/50.

Well, it's not 50/50, it's 100/100.

We are always with ourselves. We see and feel 100% of everything we do ourselves. What we don't see, and can't possibly see, is everything anyone else is feeling or doing 100% of the time.

You probably only see about half of what your partner is seeing or doing.

That means you need to perceive you're doing twice as much as what you perceive your partner is doing in order to be making an equal contribution.

By taking care of the needs of your spouse, your partner, or your best friend, you're both taking care of 100%.

When both partners do this, both will feel like their needs are being met. You'll find the spiritual connection and intimacy that so many couples don't have because they're not taking care of each other.

When you become omni-focused, you see the big picture and understand more.

It becomes more than just about you and your needs and wants.

It becomes about the other person as well.

You look at what is best for the relationship, not the individual.

> *When I started focusing on my wife's needs instead of my needs, my needs started being met at a higher level than they'd ever been before.*

The C Word

You can't control or fix other people.

However, you can influence people. The best way to influence people is with the C-Word, Communication. Here's something I've found that works for me.

When I start to feel that my wife is not as nice as I think she should be, I look at myself first. I take some time and separate myself from the situation.

I look at myself and wonder, "How have I been this week? Have I been focused on the family? Have I been doing things that are helpful? Have I been responding in a bad way? How's my attitude?"

I go through a checklist. 99% of the time I find that I'm the one that caused the issue. It's 100% my responsibility.

And you know what? When I realize it's me, most of the time just my realization that it's me fixes the situation.

Without the self-check first, things often turn to conflict. The battle begins and the relationship suffers. If this pattern continues, the relationship fails.

Tolerance And Performance

My good friend, Richie Dolan, says,

"High tolerance equals low performance. Low tolerance equals high performance."

Great Quote!!

This is where the C word comes in again. Communication.

> *When I no longer feel I can tolerate certain behavior from my partner, I check myself first. Only after I look at myself do I approach the topic with my partner and share what's bothering me.*

I ask, is this a good time for us to talk about a concern that I have?

When you have something that's bothering you, set aside time to talk so you can focus on the conversation.

It's important to have the conversations, but it's also important to create the best environment possible for the conversations.

"I'm being bothered by this. How can we fix this? Is there something I can do myself?"

Ask first about what you could do about the issue. You don't want negative things in your relationship to continue because your relationship will suffer. It's better to address the issues and look for ways they can be resolved with communication.

Winners Are Losers In Arguments

Once a battle begins, no one wins.

Especially if you have children.

Think about the effect fighting has on your kids.

As I've mentioned, I come from a broken home. I don't remember my parents being together, but I do remember the fighting. I also remember the conflicts between my stepparents and my parents.

As a kid, this has a big impact on you.

I got into a lot of fights as a kid. As a kid, I always thought I wasn't the one starting the fights. It was always someone else's fault. Looking back, I may have been, just maybe, the culprit.

If someone didn't want to listen to me, or didn't see it my way, then we were fighting. I didn't take shit from anyone.

That is not the way to be. When you get upset or agitated, it takes you out of your game.

Why would you want to do that to yourself?

When you're more concerned about being right than you are about the health of the relationship, you might win the battle, but you'll lose the war.

Instead, find ways to express gratitude with those you're in relationships with (partners, kids, friends, etc.). Share what you want in life and listen to what they want.

This is a proven way to be happier and get more out of life.

Build An Indestructible Relationship

Relationships have challenges. Some challenges will be easy to overcome, others will be difficult. Some challenges will be huge setbacks.

The question you have to ask yourself is, are you going to quit when it gets bad or are you going to turn those setbacks into ROCKET FUEL. If you want an indestructible relationship, you need to be able to turn setbacks into lessons and learning, and into ROCKET FUEL.

How do you do that?

ROCKET FUEL

I often talk about going into orbit, getting away from Earth's gravitational pull.

To me, gravitational pull reminds me of somebody or something trying to pull me down, pull me away from my goals and dreams. I want to get away from that gravity.

Here's how to do it.

Boost Your Relationships

We all have our ups and downs.

The only thing I know that can get you into orbit is ROCKET FUEL.

To get to orbit, you've got to turn these lessons learned, these setbacks, into ROCKET FUEL for your future. When you do, you'll watch your relationships flourish.

Take the issues that would normally cause a relationship to have challenges and convert those into ROCKET FUEL to thrust your relationship forward.

It's a proven system. It works.

This is what I focus on all the time and this is what you should focus on as well.

Be obsessed with turning setbacks into ROCKET FUEL.

The ABC'S Of The C Word

Remember, high tolerance, low performance and low tolerance, high performance.

Many people are afraid to communicate when they feel there is a conflict in a relationship. They shy away from confronting it, yet they will continue to complain about it.

They won't do anything to change the situation. They sweep it under the rug and don't know how to approach it until it blows up. This is the worst thing you can do when you're trying to build a relationship.

Communication, the C word I keep going back to, is of the utmost importance.

It isn't just communicating; it's communicating with your partner at the right time and in the right way.

Take Responsibility

It's easy to blame your partner, but no success ever comes from blaming. Anybody that falls into the trap of blaming the other person will see their own success falter.

Your mood and tone will go down. Your results will go down.

It's not a good place to be. To the degree you give up responsibility, you give up control.

Even if you disagree, or feel there's no way it's your fault, it will benefit you to take responsibility anyway. When you do, you'll see your relationships take off.

Don't Confuse The Two C's

Some people confuse the two C's - you know, Communication and Complaining.

Complaining is a one-way street while communication is a two-way street.

COMPLAIN

verb

express dissatisfaction or annoyance about something.

COMMUNICATE

verb

share or exchange information, news, or ideas

When you express dissatisfaction without a solution, or without asking for help with a solution, that is called complaining. Proper communication is different. This is true in any relationship at home, at work, or with friends.

There are right and wrong ways to communicate. If you generally get a negative response from people when you express your views on something, maybe you're not communicating it in the best way. Perhaps you should work on how you communicate so it doesn't sound like complaining. You want to show that you want to work together to reach a common goal.

You need to think about what you're doing and think about how you will communicate. Think about being in the other person's shoes.

Understand what the role is that you have in the undesirable responses you get from others.

Learn To Learn

Life is full of lessons.

You can either learn from lessons, or not. If not, you will have hardships and conflict in your life because you will be too busy being right rather than learning from the lesson that life is trying to teach you.

When you're in conflict, or experiencing a setback, this is the time when you feel the most hopeless, the most emotions.

The further away you get from a setback or let-down, the better you feel. You recognize the lessons in the setbacks that are there to help you grow.

Don't ever forget that the bigger the setback, the further it will propel you forward. Think of it as pulling a rubber band back. The further you pull it back, the more force it has once you let it go.

Dream Big, Be Indestructible

If you're not having setbacks or failures, you're not trying hard enough.

Your goals and visions aren't big enough. You're just lying low, being okay and mediocre.

When you become a successful person there will be pressure and stress.

Being mediocre doesn't mean less stress. There's still stress being mediocre, it's just different stress. It's the stress of trying to survive.

Doesn't it get tiring spending all that energy just trying to survive?

I hope you want more for yourself.

In the long run, it takes less energy to be indestructible and have massive success than it takes to be mediocre.

So when you approach setbacks, acknowledge them. Then take immediate action, looking for an opportunity. Ask yourself, what can I learn here? How can I turn this to my advantage? Acknowledgement followed by action changes everything.

Live On ROCKET FUEL

I want you to become indestructible. I'm sharing my thoughts on relationships because I care about you. I want your relationships to last. Your relationships at work, business, and at home. I want to see your marriages flourish. That's what this is all about.

It's impossible to become unstoppable if you're not maintaining great relationships. It's a distraction from greatness.

Let's get this movement going. Let's fill our relationships with ROCKET FUEL and launch into orbit and beyond!

CHAPTER 10

Stronger Through Adversity

"Refuse to be the victim."
- Avery Warner

Father's Day, June 2014

We were heading north on a dual lane highway just outside of Selbyville, Delaware. My wife and I were in the front. My mom was in the back seat with our kids. Our kids love my mom almost as much as I do. They call her Crazy Mom Mom because she is always goofy and fun to be around. The kids had fallen asleep, exhausted, after a fun day on the beach.

I spotted a minivan entering the highway from my left. They hadn't stopped at the stop sign entering the highway and they were coming across the southbound lanes and didn't look like they were going to stop before entering my lane.

I remember saying to my wife, "Are they going to stop?"

I slowed down to about 40 mph and moved from the left lane to the right lane to give us some extra space if they came into the northbound lanes.

They didn't stop… They came across into the northbound lanes and the space I gave wasn't enough.

We're Going To Be Alright

They hit us at the rear driver's side door.

The impact turned us sideways and then all hell broke loose.

I remember thinking, this can't be happening to us.

I'm not going out like this. I was thinking of my friend that had died in a car accident just days earlier.

It was the most violent thing I've ever felt.

Our car started rolling and I kept saying, "We're going to be alright. We're going to be alright."

I had no idea what was going to happen.

We rolled three times.

It was the longest 30 seconds of my life. So many things went through my mind in that short amount of time. I became aware of how powerful our brains are.

Here are a few of the many thoughts that went through my head during that short 30 seconds between impact and when we stopped:

OMG he hit us.

We are going to be ok. Are we going to be ok?

What's happening? Are we rolling over?

Please don't hit anything else. Please don't hit anything else.

There is no way my kids can survive this violent motion.

Oh no, the roof is caving in. Please don't crush us!

God, please save us.

Upside Down

When the truck came to a stop, we were in shock.

I immediately started pressing on the horn. I was thinking, I need to get attention so that no one hits us. The air was thick with the smell of burning metal, rubber, and plastic. I remember intense pressure on my lap and chest.

I was so afraid to look over at Jen, let alone turn around to look at the kids. I didn't know if they'd be alive, or even in the car. The accident had been so violent, I was sure they did not survive.

It wasn't until I looked at Jen that I came to my senses and realized we were upside down. The pressure on my chest and lap was my seatbelt holding me up. Jen was so quick to unbuckle her seatbelt. She fell onto the roof that was covered in broken glass. I remember it cutting her hands as she crawled back to see if the kids were ok. I turned around and saw that everyone was conscious and alive! They were shaken and hanging upside down, but they were alive.

The windows had been blown out. Glass was everywhere. Someone was yelling, "Come out over here!"

Nick was helping my mom unbuckle while Jen was unbuckling Sophie. Jen helped Sophie down and handed her through the shattered window to a man outside the truck.

Slowly, everyone crawled out. I was the last one to exit. I couldn't believe what I saw. The debri field looked like a war zone. Glass and metal were everywhere. Our beach gear, cooler, food, soda, and everything else that had been in our truck was littered up and down the highway.

I looked back at the truck and could not believe what I saw.

It was a large, mangled mass of steel.

We Were So Lucky

People kept asking us how many people had been in the truck. Everyone assumed at least one person had been thrown from the truck because of how bad the accident had been.

I walked to the side of the road to where my family members were all being worked on by the EMT's. Everyone seemed alert and ok.

I was so grateful.

I felt like I had won the Superbowl.

The only other time I had felt like that was when my kids were born.

I literally jumped into the air and celebrated. The witnesses probably thought I was crazy, but I felt a need to celebrate after such a traumatic and unreal experience. The EMTs immobilized everyone except for me. It was a precaution for the ride to the hospital. They told me I was going to ride in my son's ambulance with him, but they loaded Nick up and took off without me.

We started to panic. We thought maybe they realized there was something wrong with Nick and had to get him to the hospital asap.

I jumped into the front seat of the girls' ambulance and told the driver to find out what happened. He radioed them and they said it was just a miscommunication. They had thought I wasn't going to the hospital.

After knowing Nick was ok, the ride in the ambulance was exhilarating. We were going 90 mph and all the while I was hollering back to the girls, checking to see how they felt.

We pulled up to the hospital and I ran in to find Nick. He was chilling in a room in the ER. All good. We were all so lucky. We had some minor injuries, but physically we were in pretty good shape.

Mentally, it was another story.

PTSD is real.

When I'm Weak, I'm Strong

That night, we were back at our home. All I wanted to do was hole up in our bedroom and have the whole family in our bed. I had a weird feeling. I started having thoughts of guilt. I really felt like I let my family down. I felt like I should have been able to avoid it. How could I have allowed my family to experience something like that? These were all false feelings, but they were real.

I analyzed every possible way I could have avoided the collision. The only answer seemed to be if I had left at a different time, but how could I have known?

They were very confusing thoughts and feelings…

Here is what I wrote on a Facebook post after that accident..

> *"A father is supposed to be able to protect his family.*
> *I felt totally helpless on Sunday, Father's Day.*
>
> *The irony is, our Father, the one in Heaven, did protect our family on His day. So, I read this verse that morning and it really opened my eyes, and I couldn't help sharing it so that maybe it will help you.*
>
> *2 Corinthians 12:10 ERV*
>
> *Yes, I'm glad to have weaknesses if they are for Christ.*
>
> *I'm glad to be insulted and have hard times.*
>
> *I'm glad when I'm persecuted and have problems, because it is when I'm weak that I'm really strong."*

Push Into Fear And Difficulties

The anxiety I experienced while driving for the next couple of weeks was ridiculous. When I drove, I stayed way over to the right on the shoulder and drove very slowly.

I was literally paranoid that someone was going to come across the center line or run an intersection.

The accident resulted in a feeling that I needed to be in control of everything. Shortly after the accident, I had to take a trip which involved flying.

I was a mess.

I started to feel a sense of panic as I was checking my bags at the airport.

This anxiety grew as I went through security and boarded the plane. My mind went to crazy places.

I kept telling myself, "You got this," and, "What are you made of?"

The formula I used to get through this and drive and fly again without panicking is something I've used in my life ever since.

My formula for busting out of this was to push into it. Go all out. Drive as much as I can, fly as many times as I can. The bumpier the flight, the better.

I started to thrive on leaning into fears and anything that made me anxious.

I didn't want to feel like a victim.

Nothing was going to stop me again.

And guess what? It worked. It destroyed any sense of panic or fear.

I started sharing this with people.

It was like a super-power. I couldn't keep the success to myself.

I have used this super-power ever since.

Relationships Are Everything

Lean into communication with spouses, partners, friends, kids, etc.

When you have a concern, share it. I realized that people who care about you in life want to know how you're feeling. Nobody wants to have tension in relationships.

A top cause of failure in relationships is poor communication.

If you commit to having open and honest conversations, it opens you up to deeper, more loyal, and fulfilling relationships.

Take Full Responsibility

"It's like a horror story, he's stealing from all of us!"

Those were the words I heard over the phone that confirmed my suspicions.

Relationships can evolve in many directions, like cars on the highway.

We spent seven years building a business under the owner of a mortgage company. Our division started out with just two of us, myself and one of my best friends from childhood, Chris Short.

Over those seven years, we slowly added one good person at a time. We were learning as we went, because neither one of us had run a business before. We went from one branch to two and then eventually six mortgage branches.

We were closing over $150 million in loan volume and thought we had made it.

We stopped growing. We got comfortable and the only thing we grew was complacent.

Another mistake we made was trusting without confirming. We trusted people with critical parts of the business without double checking what they were doing. We found out money was being stolen from our business. By the time we found out, they had stolen a lot of money - to the tune of over a million dollars.

These two mistakes led us to hit rock bottom in our business.

I take full responsibility for what happened.

If we had kept growing and taken things to the next level, we would not have been impacted as bad. If we had insisted on being shown information, or done the research ourselves, we would have caught the fact that we were being taken advantage of a lot sooner.

> *No matter what happens to you in life, good or bad,*
> *you must take 100% responsibility.*
>
> *You always have an impact on what happens to you,*
> *or at least how big of an impact it has on you.*

Change Your Point Of View

The Overview Effect is a cognitive shift in awareness experienced by astronauts during spaceflight while viewing the Earth from outer space. It's a dramatic change of perception experienced from a change in point of view.

Two siblings have the same drug addict parents.

One turns into a drug addict because his parents were drug addicts.

ROCKET FUEL

One becomes massively successful because his parents were drug addicts.

Which one are you?

Do you see adversity as something negative or as something positive?

When we first had to start over in my business, I thought it sucked.

A year later I thought it was the greatest thing ever.

What we are building now is bigger, better, and more rewarding than anything before. If I had to start over again, I wouldn't be afraid. I know what I'm made of.

I often reflect on things I wanted to happen in my past that never came to fruition.

To quote a song from Garth Brooks, "Sometimes I thank God for unanswered prayers."

Are there things that aren't going your way, no matter how hard you try?

That agent that I wanted to do business with that seemed like a perfect situation.

That employee I was recruiting for that never came aboard.

That trip I wanted to take that just never fit in the schedule.

That girl that moved on from a relationship I thought I wanted.

All these things happened, or didn't happen, for a reason. They would have altered the course of my destiny.

Some of them might have made things easier at the time, but easier is not always better. When things don't go your way and times get tough, it makes you stronger and better. It leads you to a destination that is bigger, more satisfying, and more successful. I've experienced this many times.

My life is now better than anything I ever wanted in the past. Looking back, I can see everything that happened to me got me to where I am today.

> *When things don't go your way, change your point of view.*
> *When you don't like the results, know that you're being put on a*
> *path to train and prepare you for something bigger and better.*

Other's Invisible Journeys

One day when we were in New York, we ran into Mike Rowe. Mike is the host of Discovery Channel's, Dirty Jobs.

We got into a conversation and I asked him to share a mistake he made on his path to success. I told him I liked to learn from other's mistakes to speed up my own journey to success.

His response really hit me.

He said, "Mistakes, wow, we've had many."

Wow! I knew everyone had their own road to travel, but I hadn't ever really thought about looking back at the challenges successful people had gone through to get to their success.

What obstacles did they face?

How long did it take to get to where they are?

Don't assume successful people just fell into their fate.

Everyone has their own journey.

Everyone's journey is filled with lessons that got them to where they are.

If you're fortunate enough to run into someone successful, instead of trying to get a selfie or an autograph, why not ask them about their journey?

Find out their story and what they are made of.

You will likely find it is not what you initially thought.

What Makes You Stronger

We survive tough times because we don't give up. No matter how long it takes, we push through to get to the other side.

ROCKET FUEL

But I want more. I never want to just survive. If you look for it, there's always a way to survive AND convert the challenge into ROCKET FUEL to propel us higher.

> *I've been through many tough times in my 44 years.*
>
> *What I want to share with you is how to get through difficult times more quickly and with as little damage as possible.*

BE AWARE

Take a moment to assess what it is you're going through.

Be clear with yourself that you CAN and WILL make it through.

Eliminate any feelings of being a victim and tell yourself you're built to withstand this.

Remember RULE #1 - Convert all setbacks, difficulties, negative people, etc., into ROCKET FUEL for your future.

BUCKLE DOWN

Get regimented.

Have your day structured so you know what you're doing. This will keep you focused and keep you from dwelling on the circumstances.

Start with a morning routine. My morning routine goes like this:

> *Wake up EARLY and have a moment of gratitude.*
>
> *Write down a few things I'm thankful for. Pray, meditate, and get my thoughts together.*
>
> *I write down my goals. I make them big and specific. I write them as if they've already happened.*
>
> *Read for 10 minutes. I try to make it something that inspires me.*
>
> *After a healthy breakfast, I hit the gym.*

Get to work! While at work, reach for the stars. Go out of your way to go further than you do when things are going well. Aim to help and lift-up others.

BE CONSISTENT

Follow your routine. Be persistent no matter how long it takes to get through the struggle.

As long as you keep going, you will not succumb to your circumstances.

You will always come out stronger on the other side.

CHAPTER 9

Leading From The Rooftops

"Rise to the top."
- Joe Vargas, @hustler on IG

You Are Great

To be a great leader, you can't be worried about being liked. You can't rely on others to make your dreams come true.

You must believe you are great before anyone else will.

You may want to go to others for help or support, but, when you share big dreams with others, don't expect validation or encouragement. Most people will project their own fears onto you. You can't listen to them or their fears.

These reactions are a reflection of their own beliefs, often because they are reminded of their own failures or how they quit on their own dreams.

They stopped believing they were great, or never thought that they were to begin with.

Know that you are great and that you can do big things. As a great leader for your company, it's imperative to get people engaged and inspired. If you can't get them on board, let them go from your company immediately. Disengaged and uninspired people are the number one killers of companies. These people are dangerous because they don't care about you or the company. They are there for a job and paycheck and nothing more.

As a leader, you should be looking and watching for this intently. It's not hard to spot disengaged employees. You should talk about your vision and company culture often.

Be Driven, Be Valuable

A marginal effort will never lead to success.

Marginal people produce marginal results.

Be a maniac with passion and effort.

When you are driven, every obstacle in front of you will be destroyed. In everything that you do, try to be a case study for success. At work, at home, and in all your relationships.

You want your team to feel like they belong to the greatest company in the world.

Be engaged with them and help them. You will get great results when you do.

Make yourself as valuable as possible to your relationships.

To your family, spouse, kids…

To your friends…

To your employer, company, to your employees…

Be the person that you would want to be friends with.

Be the person you would want as a parent, spouse, or child.

Be the employee you would want to hire. The boss you would want to work for.

Leading From The Roof

I'm going to share a little story that hits home with me.

I call it leading from the roof.

It's about a guy named Scott Mann, a Green Beret who fought in Afghanistan.

Scott and his team of Green Berets were there to help defeat the Taliban. They would go into Afghan villages and the people would be paralyzed in fear of the Taliban.

Scott and his team would make three promises to the villagers.

The Three Promises

Number one: If the villagers wanted the Green Berets to leave, they would leave.

Number two: If the villagers wanted the Green Berets to stay, they would stay. Staying would mean it would get worse before it got better.

Number three: When the Taliban attack, Scott and his team will be on the roofs fighting to protect the villagers whether or not the villagers came to help.

Up On The Roof

Can you relate to this story in your own life? I know I can.

I went through something like this in the business world. I had success by using this type of leadership without understanding why it worked until I read this story.

It hit me like a ton of bricks.

The Green Berets would go up on the roofs by themselves and fight all night. In the morning, they would come down carrying their dead and injured comrades. This sometimes went on for weeks.

Then something would start to happen, something crazy.

One villager, then two, then many started to join them on the roof to fight alongside the Green Berets.

Working together with the Green Berets, the villagers started kicking the Taliban's ass.

When the villagers saw the commitment and sacrifice of the Green Berets, they wanted to join them. The example of the Green Berets moved the villagers out of their paralysis of fear. They moved from fear to fighting like lions, to fighting like their lives depended on it.

The Green Berets are some of the toughest people on earth, but, rather than forcing the villagers to work with them, they led them by example and earning trust.

I share this story because the concept carries over to life and business. I had a relatable experience with our mortgage business. Back in February 2018, we had to make a change. We had to leave the company we had worked under for almost twelve years. Sometimes things happen that are out of our control and the only thing we can control is our response. We didn't want to leave, what happened wasn't our choice and everyone was paralyzed from taking action.

My Three Promises

I had 22 employees look at me and say, "Now what? What are we going to do?" They were in shock and paralysis. So was I.

I know many of you can relate. You're not alone. We all go through these types of situations.

I didn't stay paralyzed for long. I thought, "This isn't what I'm made of."

I remembered telling my team three things. It's crazy how similar they are to what Scott told his team and they're one of the reasons Scott's story hit home so hard for me. My three promises:

Promise number one: If you don't want to be here, you can leave.

Promise number two: It will get a lot tougher before it gets better.

Promise number three: I want everyone to come on this journey, but we are going to make this work with or without you.

I laid out our strategy and the vision of what we were going to do. I invited them to be a part of it if they wanted to. I explained it would get tougher before getting better. I asked for their alignment and commitment if they decided to come with us. I told them I wanted them to be a part of it, but that we were going to make it happen either way.

I repeated this many times. I felt this with conviction deep down inside.

I told them, "Look around. Some of the people here right now are not going to make it. Some people are not going to be here a few months from now."

I know our situation wasn't like the Green Berets by any means. I know I wasn't in a war zone, but psychologically I was handling this like a life-or-death situation. I still have strong emotions from that time even years later.

Of course, I got a little hell from it.

Some of my employees didn't like that I said we were going to do it with or without them.

I told them, "Guys, look, I will do this myself if I have to, because I know I can. But I promise you, if you get on board and commit, there are going to be some huge victories and we are going to change people's lives.

There will be hurdles. It will be tough. You're going to need to step up your game to make it. Some people aren't going to be up for the challenge. Others will not support you. You'll need to push through.

If this doesn't work, we will help you if you want to leave. We will help you find another job. We don't wish anything bad on anyone.

We have a vision and we are moving in the direction of that vision. We can't have salmon swimming upstream on us. It just doesn't work."

One of the biggest mistakes I've made in my life has been keeping people around too long. People that were acting like salmon, swimming upstream and causing the river not to flow properly. I don't like to give up on people, even if they give up on themselves, but, if you don't take action, it can pull you backwards.

I was constantly on the phone telling everyone, "Listen, we have to make a certain amount of calls per day. We need to call our referral partners because the biggest hurdle for salespeople is not being top-of-mind."

I would make calls to referral partners to show the team that it wasn't as hard or scary as they made it out to be. I did this with consistency sharing the results and showing off about what I was doing. Leading from the rooftops.

Soon one person jumped in, then another, and soon the whole team had come together, taking massive action and getting the results we had been looking for.

The Snowball Effect

People's reactions to what I was doing were not always positive, but, with consistency and persistence, people started buying in.

I talk about the snowball effect all the time. When a snowball starts to roll, it gets bigger and gains momentum. The bigger it gets, the faster it rolls, and the harder it is to stop. Everybody starts feeding off each other.

I was doing these activities and people saw it. It became a snowball rolling downhill.

We started breaking records. Not every month, but consistently more and more. Yes, the economy has helped, but our hard work put us in the right place to capitalize on it.

The power of our activities, attitudes, and culture were big drivers. When everybody started buying in, we began seeing wins and celebrating them.

I use the snowball analogy often. I believe our growth and culture continues to grow like an unstoppable snowball.

We have to maintain it. We still have to work, but becoming unstoppable is the motto and mindset of our organization.

Rooftop Leadership

"I'm doing my best." I'm sure you've heard someone say this before. The truth is, none of us are ever doing our best. We can always do better.

To get in that space of continuing to do better, you need to have something that drives you. A story or an experience that you can convert into ROCKET FUEL to propel you forward.

I never realized until I heard Scott's story that rooftop leadership was a part of our culture. Rooftop leadership is what it took to get our "village" back from the dark place we were in.

Many people were scared and anxious. There were a lot of uncertainties. I'm thankful everyone bought into the vision that we put in front of them and came along for the journey.

The People-Building Business

Getting a home loan is a big deal for people, but we go beyond that.

We are in a people-building business.

We want to change people's lives, help them reach their potential, and push to greatness. We take great pride in it. I think this passion helps us push through the hard times of building a business and helps us become unstoppable..

ROCKET FUEL

CHAPTER 8

ROCKET FUEL For Champions

"Release your Inner Champion"
- Dana Cavalea

Take Care Of Yourself

You can't take on the world if you can't take care of the two square feet around you. I'm all about being proactive in preparing for future setbacks, difficulties, and letdowns. The cleaner the fuel, the greater the thrust.

You must think of your body in this way. To prepare yourself to be able to handle anything, your mind and your body must be a priority. I believe that the foundation of a successful, healthy, and happy life starts with taking care of your mind and body.

You must want to be a champion and do what it takes to be a champion.

"Champions are champions before they're champions."
- *Dave Austin*

It's clear that you want to be a champion because you've read this far.

It's important to understand that you need to strive toward your potential in all areas of your life, not just a few. When you neglect one area, it starts to pull down the other areas. I have witnessed this in my life and in countless others.

In my life, there have been times when I focused solely on my profession and finances, letting my diet and exercise suffer. I became sluggish, anxious, and even depressed. Despite the successes I was experiencing in my business and my finances, I wasn't happy because my health was suffering.

In football, working out and eating right are imperative to avoid injury. While I was in college playing football, I ate enough to fuel me, but it wasn't always clean fuel. My success could have been much greater if I had focused on better health and on paying better attention to what I was putting in my body.

After my football career was over, the partying and poor health habits continued for almost all of my twenties. I ate poorly, drank, and rarely exercised. My finances, profession, and health all suffered through that decade and a lot of it stemmed from not focusing on keeping my body in top shape.

Before helping others, you must take care of yourself.

It's never beneficial in the long run to take care of others at the expense of your health.

I got up to 235 pounds. I didn't realize how fat and out of shape I was. I remember feeling out of breath going up a set of stairs in my early 30s. My back was hurting, and I had pain in my knees. I was deteriorating.

In 2014, I committed to making a change. I remember telling myself, "Enough is enough."

I committed to being an animal and to getting into the best shape of my life. I embarked on a journey to not just get in shape physically, but also mentally. I started telling myself I was an absolute beast and I needed to start acting like one. Every day I would wake up and tell myself mantras like, "unleash the beast," and, "you are an animal."

The more I started believing it, the more I started acting like it in the gym and with my diet.

You Can Do It

After my near-fatal car accident with my family, I started learning physical exercises that I didn't like doing. I came to the realization that I didn't like them because I either wasn't good at them or because I was weak in the muscles used for that particular exercise.

For example, burpees. I hated them, so I started doing them every day. I leaned in and soon I could do more burpees in a minute than anyone at our gym. I thought running was boring, so I forced myself to run and figure out ways to make it interesting.

Before you know it, I was up to running seven miles every time I ran, and I was loving it.

The same went for Crossfit workouts. I leaned in so hard that I'd feel like dying, then I'd push harder to prove to myself I could do it. Each time I hit a milestone, I became addicted to hitting the next level. I never wanted to go back to where I was before.

> *Leaning into things makes you a badass.*
>
> *Your confidence goes through the roof.*
> *It's a monstrous mental toughness builder.*
>
> *You feel like you can take on the world.*

I had two young children when I started working out. I remember thinking to myself how selfish it was of me that I hadn't started working out sooner. My kids deserved to have me around to see them grow and to hopefully see their kids grow. I also want to be the best version of myself for my wife and my employees.

> *It's important to understand that when you don't take*
> *care of yourself, you also are not taking care of others.*
> *If you don't feel like working out, if you don't feel like eating*
> *healthy, the effect is not just on you. Your choices affect every-*
> *one around you and everyone who relies on you.*
> *Once you get this mindset, it's easier to commit to doing*
> *the things to take care of yourself and to be a champion.*

The Next Level

When you push yourself to your limits, you really find out what you're made of. When I started working out, my competitive juices started flowing again in a way they hadn't since my days of playing college football. I began feeling great. I began pushing myself so hard in the gym that I would start to notice that things outside of the gym were easier. Things that had previously made me want to quit no longer held me back. I would keep pushing through.

When I pushed my limits in the gym, I started to realize that my mind would try to get me to quit while my body still had plenty left. We are designed for survival and our brains are there to give warning. But, when our internal warning light comes on, it's like being low on gas. You still have 30 to 40 miles left. And it's that 30 to 40 miles left that is the space for 10x growth.

This translates into all aspects of life, including business and relationships.

I learned that I could push past that point and find massive success. It gave me a huge advantage over those that were not pushing themselves at the gym. They didn't realize how much further they could go past that first warning sign. They didn't realize how much growth they were leaving on the table.

Confidence is the result of achievement. The confidence I found in the gym carried over into all parts of my life. This is an amazing feeling.

Nothing happens overnight. Big results in the gym, like in everything great, come from consistent actions over long periods of time. Don't begin working out and expect to see a difference in the mirror after the first day. Commit to consistently doing the work and I promise you'll see the results. You'll be a different person physically, spiritually, and mentally.

Eat For Fuel

Dieting was another area I needed to push hard.

When I began eating clean and focusing on diet, I really noticed the reactions and words of other people.

I spoke about this earlier.

When you start to improve and elevate yourself, others feel threatened.

You will hear comments and sense attitudes of resentment from others. This happens because those people know they should be doing more with their own diet and exercise. They justify their failure by throwing digs, making comments, or having a resentful attitude towards you.

It's important to be aware of this because it stops many people from pushing forward in their journey to get in better shape and become healthier.

There were more than a few comments made when I brought in healthy, homemade lunches and told coworkers I wasn't going out to lunch with them.

Even people close to you will do this. Be prepared and know how to handle it. Know that the best thing you can do is to persist and show them the results.

I started forcing myself to get uncomfortable. I leaned into the patient part of dieting. It's all about consistency over time. I stopped eating for taste and shifted my mindset into eating for fuel. I kept telling myself that what I was eating was either building me or tearing me down.

I got down to 187 pounds. I was shredded. I had no clothes that fit me and felt the best I've ever felt in my life.

Before I had this transformation myself, I used to think that the before and after pictures on the Internet were either photoshopped or done with some sort of drugs.

My mind would try to justify why I couldn't look like that.

> *Often those that cry "scam" are the ones that are not willing to put in the work commitment and dedication.*

Maybe you've told yourself things like, "I don't really need to look that muscular, or that cut up." I know I have.

What you're doing is giving yourself an out. You're letting yourself off the hook. I can say this because I've been there.

I can help you.

The feeling you get when you hit your physical and health goals is hard to put into words. You feel amazing and your confidence goes through the roof.

You feel like you can take on the world.

Professionally, it made me an animal. I've always been a hard worker and a "get-stuff-done" kind of guy, but now I leaned into areas I had shied away from in the past.

I forced myself to talk to anyone who was around me wherever I was. I had a goal of just connecting with people.

Before I knew it, I'd developed a huge network. Asking for business became easy.

My first question was always, "How can I help you?" It works. Caring about others helps others care for you.

I stopped pushing off problems and instead jumped all over them.

I totally eliminate the part where you let things run wild in your head. Most of the thoughts in our heads are imaginary anyway.

You can fix any problem when you address it quickly and head on.

Take the emotion out of it.

I became the guy that others come to to fix problems. I love it.

Leaders are the ones that others go to for insight and support.

My money situation improved because I was not scared anymore.

I started spending on nice things because I had confidence in my ability to earn more money. It's a truly game changing mindset.

Become An Inspiration

It's important to understand that others are always watching. People watch other people to compare themselves and validate their position in life.

Something that is truly underestimated when accomplishing something for yourself, especially when it's outward facing, is the impact you have and the inspiration you are to others.

By not excelling, you are limiting the advancement of those around you. When others are complacent, those around them often become complacent because they're no longer threatened. This keeps them all from advancing.

Do it for more than just yourself. Add the motivation that those you care about are watching you. Don't eat clean and get in shape just for yourself. Do it for those you love. This will give you more ROCKET FUEL to push through discomfort. Make it your nonnegotiable duty and obligation to be in the best shape of your life. Be an inspiration to those around you.

Be Fearless

Make a commitment to yourself right now to lean into hard things for 30 days. It doesn't need to be a traumatic experience.

Anything that scares you, push into it.

Anything you haven't acted on, lean into it.

If you've delayed because you don't know something, force yourself to learn it.

Find a mentor, read, watch videos.

These are life changing tactics. Not only will they help you, but they will impact everyone around you.

Fearless is the best way to describe it.

CHAPTER 7

Forget Plan B

"People perform better when there is no safety net."
- Arnold Schwarzenegger

Stuck

I've always wanted to live near the ocean. It drove my choice of college and it drove my choice of where we built our home. During the early years of our marriage, we lived in a rural area of Delaware. I know a lot of people love living there, but, for me, it felt boring and uninspiring. I felt stuck.

There were several reasons to stay in Delaware. I have wonderful and supportive in-laws who lived across the street from us there. They are amazing and they were there for anything we needed. It was very comfortable and convenient. As much as I appreciate everything they do for us, this scenario made it easy to not take risks and to fall into complacency.

Have you ever thought about living in a different city because it may give you the ability to advance your career or make a better life for you and your family? Did you move or did you stay? Did you decide to stay where you are because, "It's where I'm from," or, "I can't move away from my family," or, "I'm comfortable."

I know this is a sensitive topic.

You may disagree with my point of view.

Here are some things to consider.

According to a poll done in 2020 by Market Watch, 70%+ of people in the US live paycheck to paycheck.

Staying in a geographical area that holds you and your family back from more financial stability is ludicrous.

Don't get me wrong, extended family is important.

However, I believe it's your obligation to do whatever you can to provide for your immediate family. I believe it's your obligation to seek abundance at a level to be able to weather any storm.

This is where most people make a huge mistake. They only go for providing just enough to get by. They feel that going for anything more than that, for abundance, is unnecessary and maybe even greedy.

When people go for abundance, they are often looked down on by others. This is a common theme in this book because it's important to understand.

Never quit going for abundance, or for anything you want, because of other's comments or resentments. It will hold you back and you will look back with regret. You will not have gotten what you wanted or gone where you wanted, because you quit over other people's hang ups.

Making excuses about why you can't relocate is just an easy way out of taking a risk, becoming uncomfortable, and making things happen.

Being Comfortable is Boring

Have you ever met a person who was doing whatever it takes to chase their dreams who was also suffering from depression? I haven't.

Depression and anxiety step in when someone lets off the gas and stops moving forward towards their purpose.

No wonder so many people are suffering from depression.

For nine years I stayed in a town where I was comfortable. Everything changed when I decided to commit to moving near the ocean and building the house of my dreams.

When I made that commitment, I had no idea how I was going to do it. I just knew I would.

My decision to move also gave my extended family an opportunity, or an "excuse," to travel to see us, lifting them out of their "boring" comfort zone.

Inspiration and motivation can be found in the people we surround ourselves with and in the different places we visit.

> Important lesson: Don't worry about the "how", just commit. Once you commit, the "how" will appear. When you put the energy towards something, the map will come to you in many ways that you couldn't see prior to your commitment.

My wife and I drove to Ocean City, MD to look for developments with the biggest houses we could find. We would look at the prices and think, there's no way we can afford this. But then we would remember we had made the commitment and we knew the way would appear.

My wife and I had to do more figuring things out. We were used to having her father take care of anything that went wrong with the house. I'm not a handyman. My wife and I had to figure it out without her father.

This made us stronger. We had to learn to survive and weather storms without that support.

I think it's important to understand this. While it's great to have a support system, there is nothing like being forced to make it on your own.

"I hate Plan B and I'll tell you why... when you start doubting yourself, that's very dangerous. What you're basically saying is that, if my plan doesn't work, I have a fallback plan... Every thought you put into Plan B is taking away thought and energy from Plan A... People perform better when there is no safety net." - Arnold Schwarzenegger

When you remove Plan B, you take yourself into uncomfortable territory.

You have no other choice but to make.

It starts to build you into an unstoppable, indestructible force.

You gain knowledge and experience that can never be taken away from you.

You start seeing yourself thriving.

So many people miss out on having the life of their dreams because they get stuck being comfortable.

Anyone who has excelled in any area of life has had to move out of their comfort zone. Having a "burn-the-ship" mentality all but guarantees success.

Grant Cardone says, "Stay broke. Go to zero."

As successful as Grant's businesses are, he always grinds like he's broke. Most people get a "nest egg" and they get comfortable and let off the gas. Then they wonder why they never get to the next level.

This often happens with salespeople. When they have a good week or a good month, they often let off the gas pedal. Instead of gaining momentum and riding the wave while they are hot, they rest on their "fat pockets". The best salespeople and businesspeople never let up. They strive to make sure their graphs have an upwards trajectory. This is what success looks like in business.

It's the same in your personal life. You should see an upward trajectory in your graphs to indicate success in those areas. When the trendline on your graph flattens out or starts to dip, it's because you let off the gas and started paying more attention to Plan B than plan A. It's the result of being comfortable and complacent.

Marriages often end up in divorce because one or both partners don't have the "burn-the-ships" mentality to make the relationship work. They may have eyes on another individual or activity that takes attention away from the spouse.

If there was a graph that measured the health of those relationships that fail, you would start to see it flatten out or start to dip before it failed. A healthy relationship would show a graph trending upwards. It all has to do with being comfortable and/or taking things for granted.

Fight Boredom

Earlier I mentioned that comfortable is boring. When you're bored, your attention can start to shift to destructive behaviors.

Did you know most people who waste money on things they don't need, or on vices like gambling, drinking, and drug abuse, are often suffering from boredom.

I know this from experience. I don't need to do research. I've seen it in myself. I've seen it in friends, coworkers, and family. I've seen businesses destroyed, marriages and families ruined, and friendships lost.

Boredom stems from a lack of purpose.

We need purpose. We crave stimulation.

Problems come when you're not intentional about your purpose.

Without clarity and something that challenges us, we will often turn to negative things to stimulate us, including over eating, drugs, alcohol, gambling, promiscuity, and more. These are things that WILL NOT make you unstoppable and indestructible. They ARE NOT ROCKET FUEL.

When people refuse to leave their hometowns to explore bigger and better opportunities, they start to fall into letting life live them rather than living life.

Every day starts to have the same monotonous schedule.

When I'm bored, I use it as a trigger to produce or be creative. I find problems to solve and I have a hard time sitting still once I flip this trigger. You won't find me laying on the beach or sitting by a pool for too long, nor will you find me sitting on a couch watching TV.

Use this hack to ignite your creativity and productivity. Create a trigger now for when you start to feel bored. Don't let fear or disgust creep in. Shift those feelings to taking positive actions towards your goals of creating and building the future you want.

ROCKET FUEL

Get Motivated

I started making trips to Miami in 2018. Not for the weather... well, not just for the weather, winters in Maryland can get pretty cold.I made trips to Miami to look at boats, large houses, and tall condo buildings. I like being around nice cars and expensive designer stores. It wasn't because I wanted all those things, it was because I like seeing what's possible for someone to have.

Those trips to Miami were highly inspirational to me, just like the trips my wife and I made to look at the nice neighborhoods in Ocean City, MD. I'm the type of person that looks at people who have things I don't, or have accomplished things I haven't, and I think to myself, "if they can do it, I know I can do it." I recommend you become this way as well.

This is part of what is so powerful about traveling outside of your hometown. Your mind gets expanded and you think bigger. You grow because your belief of what's possible grows.

Look what going to the moon has done for space travel. Where do you think the space program would be if we'd never made it to the moon?

Looking back on those trips to Miami, I can see how things improved each time I went. The hotels I stayed in got nicer, the seats on the plane got better, and I spent more on the food and entertainment. It all leads back to being inspired and to my income rising exponentially.

This works for me, so I know it will work for you. Take advantage of it.

If I'd known this at a younger age, nothing would have stopped me from traveling and seeing and having bigger, better, and nicer things.

This is not meant to come off materialistic, but, if I have a choice of how I want to live, I would rather live with nicer things.

If you're OK with being complacent and doing the same things day in and day out, then this book is not for you. But, if you refuse to settle for "good enough" and you're willing to take on a "whatever it takes mindset," then you're ready to fill up with ROCKET FUEL, launch into outer space, and live the life of your dreams.

CHAPTER 6

The Path To Massive Success

"Everybody needs a coach."
- Michael Burt

When The Student Is Ready, The Teacher Will Appear

For some reason, many people resist being coached. They spend their time complaining of being a victim and trying to defend their behavior rather than seeking counsel and insight. They push away those who could help them and spend their efforts investing in negative emotions.

Why A Coach

Why is it important to have teachers, mentors, and coaches?

When we open ourselves to learning, the right coaches and mentors can give us clarity in our goals, support us towards achieving our goals, and create a structure of accountability.

In addition to direction and advice, coaches provide insight into our blindspots. This is important because it's difficult to read our own label from inside the bottle.

ROCKET FUEL

When the student is ready, the teacher will appear. I have many different coaches and mentors that help me in different areas of my life.

"The fastest and most effective way to get somewhere is to find someone who's already been there and ask for directions. Learning from our own mistakes is valuable, learning from other's mistakes is priceless."
- Chip Hopper

There's no way I would be where I am today without the coaches and mentors who have been a part of my journey. It's important to both be coached and to be a coach. This is where the real learning takes place. Here are some of the things I've found helpful for myself and for those I've coached.

Control Your Thoughts

I've been a part of both winning teams and losing teams in sports, business, and relationships. I'm obsessed with studying why we win or lose and I've discovered the fundamental causes of winning.

Your body is made up of tens of trillions of cells. It's hard to comprehend that number. These cells work as a community, directed by one central director, your brain.

So, you're not an individual, you're a community of cells. Tens of trillions of them. Talk about strength in numbers.

It's been proven that your thoughts produce energy, which sends directives to all your cells. This energy is then emitted outside of your body and is sensed by others.

Have you heard the saying he or she has good vibes? Vibes are short for vibrations.

Positive and negative thoughts are sent as vibrations. This is why it's important to control your thoughts.

Be intentional on what and how you think.

Your energy affects your surroundings without even saying a word.

I know it's hard to wrap your brain around this. When you have a thought, and your brain emits that energy to your trillions of cells, those waves are picked up by others.

I'm sure you have heard the phrase, "Thinking on the same wavelength."

When a group of people have a common belief, or are on a mission towards the same goal, the energy of the group resonates. This is so powerful.

This can work both ways.

Have you seen families, businesses, or teams that seem to have all the right pieces, but get torn apart? If you dig into it, you'll often find that those individuals were not on the same wavelength.

There are tons of examples of successful businesses and teams that, on the surface, don't appear to have the talent to be successful.. Somehow they continue to win.

All of them are thinking on the same page and their thoughts are all leading in the same direction.

This phenomenon is often referred to as "gelling," or, "clicking."

Be Positive

After knowing how your cells respond, why would you ever have a negative thought again?

The answer is, it takes work to keep positive. It's not easy.

If you are accustomed to thinking negative, all your cells have momentum in a negative direction. With trillions of them, that's some serious momentum.

You must work hard to move in the opposite direction.

Here is what you can do.

Anytime you have a negative thought, acknowledge it, understand it, and accept it. Then work to reframe it to serve you and move you back to the space of positivity where you want to be.

Then keep doing that over and over.

You will be slowing the momentum of the cells going in the wrong direction and changing their course. It takes work, but the reward of shifting your thinking in a positive direction is so big that you must do it.

It's your responsibility to yourself, your family, and the world.

Behaviors and Habits

I want you to ask yourself, "What can I do to contribute to the culture of my business, job, family, and organization?"

We can't control other people, but our tendency is to try.

When you read below, focus on what you can do to improve, not on what other people need to be doing. Human tendency is to think of what others need to fix rather than looking inward.

Don't do that!

If we focus on our own behaviors, and ONLY our own behaviors, when reading this, it will make a huge difference.

I need this reminder as much as anyone. Consider the following:

1) What attitude do I bring each day? How can I be the most valuable person in anything I'm involved in?

2) How do I do my job? How am I supposed to do my job?
   How is the way I'm doing my job affecting my teammates and family members? Am I making their jobs easier or harder?

3) How do i respond when things don't go according to plan? Do I blow my top and let it ruin my day, or do I handle myself with composure and do whatever it takes to move forward? Remember, we owe it to those around us to get the job done.

4) How am I showing up? The way I show up shows how much I care. There's a saying, "People don't care how much you know, until they know how much you care."

5) Is my focus on myself or on my team/family?

Again, this is a self reflection exercise.
We can't control others, but, when we focus on
improving ourselves, we influence those around us.

Your Surroundings

I need you to think about something.

Are the people around you lifting you up or pulling you down? Do they make you feel inspired or do they make you feel drained?

I can't stress enough how important the
people around you are to your life.

Who do you spend most of your time with?

Take inventory of the people that are around you most of the time.

Are they people striving for excellence or are they comfortable with where they are?

Are they moving in the same direction as you?

Do they support you in your vision or do they tear you down and neg you out?

These are questions you must ask yourself.

The impact the people have on you is massive.

The more you're around them, the bigger the impact.

Hanging around negative people is often a slow, gradual slide backwards that we don't realize until it's too late.

Life is short, don't waste it being around those that are not lifting
you higher, encouraging you, and supporting your goals.

Think Big

Imagine a life where everyone around you is cheering you on with positive attitudes, pushing you and supporting your vision. They celebrate your wins and accomplishments with you.

When you fall, they pick you up and tell you to get back at it. They encourage you to think big and never settle.

> *I won't slow down in putting out content
> with the purpose of helping others.*
>
> *The more hate I receive, the more times people tell me
> to slow down, the harder I'll push. Those that try to
> hold you down are often those that need the most help.*
>
> *I challenge you to join me. Lean into the haters
> and those that try to limit your reach.*
>
> *Put the right people in your inner circle.*

Here are 3 things you should do today to start living in that world:

1. Take inventory of the 5 people you spend most of your time with. Rate them. Are they pulling you up or dragging you down?

2. Avoid anyone who is pulling you down. Start looking for those that challenge you and propel you forward and up. If it's family pulling you down, confront them about it and let them know it's unacceptable. Let them read this. The truth hurts sometimes, but remember it's your life and you only have one.

3. Make this a part of your life. Be super observant of this going forward. Only spend time with those that are lifting you up or with those you believe you can lift and inspire.

*If you take these steps, difficult as they may be,
your life will be forever changed. You will take off
like a shooting star towards your vision and goals.*

*You will be on course to reach your potential
and live a happier, more fulfilling life.*

You will help and inspire everyone that encounters you.

Reach Your Potential

Success can mean a lot of different things to people. Do you view success as a requirement in your daily life? This is an important question to ask yourself.

Your answer affects every person around you.

It affects your future.

Let me tell you what success means to me.

Success is when you're constantly striving to reach your potential in 5 different areas. You must strive for your potential in all five of these areas or it will limit the success in each of the others.

SPIRITUAL

I believe in our physical bodies we have a spirit that is limitless in its potential. Having success in this area is a priority for me. It's imperative not to let anyone or anything put artificial limits on your spiritual potential.

MENTAL

Have you heard the saying, attitude is everything?

Your attitude determines the degree of potential you reach. Your attitude determines your altitude.

This, like in all other areas, must be constantly worked on and evaluated.

ROCKET FUEL

PHYSICAL

Unlike the first two areas, your physical success does have a limit.

I don't care how hard you flap your arms, you're not going to fly without the help of an apparatus. Even though physical success is limited, few people reach their potential in this area. If you have problems with your diet, lack of exercise or other vices, you must acknowledge them and then commit to change.

RELATIONSHIPS

Your relationship with yourself, your partner, kids, family, friends, and co-workers.

I try to find ways to be the MVP, Most Valuable Player, in all areas of my life. If the bed needs to be made, make it. If the dishes need to be done, do them. I look for ways to add value to my relationships. Every morning I sincerely ask my wife if there's anything I can do to support her today.

Unresolved conflicts in any of your relationships will negatively affect your success in other areas. Avoid trying to "be right." Nobody wins when two people need to be right to feel good. Imagine what your life would look like if you were to reach your potential in all of your relationships.

BUSINESS

This is simple. Whatever you do, aim to dominate and be the best.

Why else would you even bother having a business or career?

Just living to pay the bills is a recipe for disaster. You'll live paycheck to paycheck and won't ever move towards your goals. You'll live a life that is unfulfilled and lacking joy.

This is an area where you need to raise your goals to an unreasonable level and then go after them with unreasonable effort.

This is success.

Be your best!

CHAPTER 5

An Inside Job

"Heal yourself from the inside out."
- Cynthia Thurlow

Be Your Best To Be The Best

Why don't people go after being their best more often? Everybody wants to feel their best or be their best, but few actually go after it. I often refer back to my childhood because I was a very observant child. I would watch things and ask questions.

Dear Grandma

My grandmother, God rest her soul, had some issues.

Everybody has issues, and she had some emotional and mental issues. The answer I got regarding them is that she grew up in an alcoholic household.

My grandfather used to tell me a story about when he first went over to my grandmother's house to meet her parents. Her father gave him a highball glass of whiskey.

That was how my great grandfather greeted him. Alcohol was prevalent and normal in her household. I don't know many more details, but I know it wasn't the best upbringing for my grandmother. It left her with some mental issues that she was never able to escape.

There were times in my childhood when my mom and I would go to visit my grandmother. She wouldn't open the door even though she was home and knew we were there. She would be in her bedroom, depressed or suffering from some other emotional situation. It would frustrate my mom and we would leave with my mom upset.

I remember holidays where my grandmother would get in an accident, or have some other issue, because of the antidepressants and anti-anxiety pills she was on. We would always worry when the phone rang that something new might have happened to my grandmother. I would ask her why she acted the way she did, but I never got a good answer. I can only speculate on why it happened.

Some people ask me, "Why do you share this kind of stuff about your family?"

If you're thinking, I can't believe Mike is sharing this stuff about his family, here's why I do.

> Because... you know what? I'm on a mission to inspire people who
> go through these things and to help them end their suffering.
>
> The only way to create change is to talk about issues.
> The more openly we can talk about our lives and
> our situations, the more we can make an impact
> in improving our lives and the lives of others.

I think my grandmother would want me to share her story if she knew it is helping others.

You Make Me Feel Better

I remember talking to my grandmother when I was a young teenager before she passed away. I would say, "Listen, there's no excuse for how you're feeling. You're making excuses. You can choose to be happy. You just need to commit to it and do it."

She would often respond, "You know what, Mikey? Every time I talk to you, I feel so much better." Everybody called me Mikey when I was younger, but I always loved when my grandmother called me Mikey.

Her comments made me feel good. It made me feel like I was getting through to her and accomplishing something.

As I got older, I would drive to her house to visit her. Do you know what I did when she didn't answer the door? I didn't turn around and leave, instead I went around and knocked on the back window. I'd call to her and say, "Hey, come on. Come open the door. I'm not leaving until you open the door."

I felt that if I could get in there and talk with her, I could cheer her up and make her feel better. It often worked.

The End

My interactions with my grandmother went on like this until I left for college.

I was two and a half hours from her and was rarely able to see her.

I remember coming home from college one day and, when I walked into the house, my stepdad, George, said, "Hey, Mikey, your grandmother killed herself."

George was never good at filtering or softening the blow, he was always very direct.

It hit me like a ton of bricks and I fell to the floor. I couldn't believe it.

Why do people commit suicide?

Even though it wasn't rational, I started blaming myself. I wondered if I could have made a difference if I hadn't gone to college.

ROCKET FUEL

Why is it that some of us can't break free from self-defeating, self-destructive behavior?

My goal is to help more people get through these feelings. My mission is to inspire millions to turn challenges and setbacks into ROCKET FUEL. My grandmother is part of my motivation and my ROCKET FUEL. While my goal is massive, it's all worth it if it inspires even just one person.

What Are You Willing To Give Up?

I believe some people don't want to sacrifice what it takes to be the best.

This is just my observation.

I'm not a doctor, I don't have a degree.

Most people sacrifice long term gains for short term gains. It's a case of intentions versus counter intentions, and counter intentions often win.

Being our best is subjective. No matter how good we do, we can always be reaching for something better. Continuous growth and learning is the only way to continue "being our best."

The Blame Game

Many people use excuses of their situations to justify not achieving success. They talk about growing up with or around alcohol, drugs, divorce, death, discrimination, or any of many other challenges. They use the lack of things like finances, knowledge, or opportunity as reasons for not succeeding. Many of these excuses are passed down by parents and grandparents and flow down the line. Negative beliefs become accepted as reality. They think things like, I can't be the best, I'm limited, I shouldn't even bother.

I look back at an uncle I admired as a kid. He was like a big brother to me.

He struggled and struggled with alcoholism, to the point I ultimately needed to separate from him. There comes a point when you've tried and tried to help and you need to move on. I pray for my uncle and wish the best for him, but continuing to be around him became self-destructive for me because he wasn't willing to listen to counsel. We all have challenges, the difference is whether or not we are committed to overcoming them.

I think the people that are going through these things lack knowledge and data.

One thing that helps is to have a support person set them straight and say, "Hey, listen. You're playing a victim role here. You have a choice."

I think it gets blinded in their mind that they actually do have a choice of how they can feel and how they can act and how much work and effort they can put into things.

Mentors are not just for business, mentors are for personal life as well. They help you move towards your goals and are beneficial for mental health. Just like in business, mentors and coaches can help in your personal life by giving you insight and holding you accountable.

A lot of people don't think about writing down goals focusing on mental health.

It's imperative to have intentional control of your mental health. Incrementally improving it and gaining momentum, until you are able to feel your best and then help and inspire others.

CHAPTER 4

Don't Give Up Three Feet From Gold

"A dream written down with a date becomes a goal.
A goal broken down into steps becomes a plan.
A plan backed by action makes your dreams come true."
- Dr Greg Reid

Striving For Gold

One story that inspires me, and reminds me so much of my ROCKET FUEL concept, is the one told by Napoleon Hill in his book *Think and Grow Rich*. Here are a few excerpts from a chapter, titled *Three Feet from Gold*.

> *"One of the most common causes of failure is the habit*
> *of quitting when one is overtaken by temporary defeat.*
> *Every person is guilty of this mistake at one time or another."*

> "Before success comes in any man's life, he is sure to meet with much temporary defeat, and, perhaps, some failure. When defeat overtakes a man, the easiest and most logical thing to do is to quit. That is exactly what the majority of men do. More than five hundred of the most successful men this country has ever known told the author their greatest success came just one step beyond the point at which defeat had overtaken them. Failure is a trickster with a keen sense of irony and cunning. It takes great delight in tripping one when success is almost within reach."

> "Knowing that you are on the cusp of great success and persisting is one thing. Not knowing that you are that close to it, when you feel defeated, and still pushing forward anyway is what separates those that do not make it and those that do."

These excerpts trigger something inside of me.

This changed everything. It unleashed the maniac within and allowed me to go for what I wanted in life. Now when I want something, I go get it.

Get committed, burn the ships committed, and everything else takes a back seat.

You keep going with unwavering faith. Obstacles become easy and you move forward after what you want.

Napoleon Hill interviewed over 500 successful people. Imagine how many other successful people experienced the same thing. This should be enough evidence for you to do the same.

Be Clear And Committed

In earlier chapters, I talked about being clear on what you want and then being committed to it. When I want something, I stubbornly go after it with an unwavering commitment. I also look for ways to convert any obstacles that come up into ROCKET FUEL.

Since unleashing my inner animal, I've been able to accomplish anything I set my mind to achieving. There are still times I pivot after realizing a path I started down wasn't what I wanted, but my life has become one I'm designing rather than just accepting. I think it is this way for most of us.

We often get what we go after relentlessly, but we never get what we stop going after.

Be relentless.

Most people will push for something until the discomfort and pain it causes feels greater than the perceived pleasure of attaining the goal in the future. Maniacs push through that pain. They become unreasonable about it. Some would call it being obsessed.

The fact is, when you don't get something you want and you consider your efforts a failure, it means you've quit going after it. Not achieving what you want isn't a failure if you haven't quit going after it, it just means you haven't gotten there yet.

The Tough Questions

If we're not getting the results we want, we must ask ourselves the tough questions.

What do I want?

What results should I expect from my current actions?

Why did I stop going after what I want?

Did I really want it?

Did I stop because I didn't want to put in the work it would take to get that thing?

Is there something I'm unwilling to sacrifice to accomplish my goal?

Did I overvalue other's opinions and let them limit me because I was concerned with what they would think?

I'm sure you might be thinking it sounds selfish to be so committed to what I want. And, when I talk about removing all obstacles, it sounds as if it's without concern for others. There's a fine line between balancing what other's desire and limiting your own dreams for them.

I balanced this by making sure my goals and dreams are more about other people than they are about myself.

For example, writing this book is accomplishing something I want for myself, but it has more to do with my goal and mission to impact and inspire millions.

The content of this book is one way I can do that. The other way is by showing others that an ordinary guy like myself can not only write an impactful book, but can also be able to find a way to get it into the hands of millions of people. This fuels me. I know people are noticing what I'm doing. I hope I can inspire them with my actions.

People watch you to learn. They watch you to see how you overcome challenges. They watch you to see how you persist. Be their inspiration.

You may think you're not a role model, but I guarantee you are to someone. No matter who you are, your actions are seen and your words are heard.

Be aware of how important your actions are. I hope I'm never an influence for someone to quit on their goals. When you quit, it's not just about you. Quitting is a selfish act. When you quit, it affects everyone around you, including everyone you love and everyone that is counting on you.

Don't Quit

We are all only three feet from gold.

Are you going to persist long enough, and with enough belief, relentlessness, and action to find gold? Here are some ways to persist in the face of adversity.

Eliminate

Eliminate limiting factors that hold you back. This includes negative beliefs.

Sometimes this means stepping back from those that are close to you, including family, friends, and coworkers.

If people aren't nurturing your potential, then they're against you.

Everything you do, every action, decision, thought, and word, is either taking you towards where you want to go or away from it.

Assimilate

Immerse yourself with positive and inspiring information. Read books that teach you ways to do better. Learn from others mistakes and failures. Listen to podcasts, get in rooms with people who have done what you want to do. Surround yourself with people who support and push you towards your goals. Surround yourself with people and information that remind you of who you are and of your potential. Write it down. Write where you want to go and what you want to accomplish. Be clear and specific, and make it gigantic.

Execute

Refuse to quit. Attack your goals and go hard every day. Keep pushing no matter how hard it gets or how long it takes. Often things take longer than wanted or expected. That's ok. Have urgency with your actions and patience with the results. Understand that if you don't quit, you will always get closer to your potential than if you never tried. Every action is better than inaction.

CHAPTER 3

Empire Building

"You're either building an empire or destroying it"
- Elena Cardone

Backwards

I wasn't 100% sure I wanted to put this part of my life in the book. Besides my close friends, I haven't shared this part of my life with anyone.

I feel I wasted seven years of my life. I'm truly embarrassed with some of the things I did during that time, including drugs and alcohol. I treated people poorly and really slid backwards in my life.. If it weren't for meeting my wife, who knows what could have happened to me. I don't want young people reading this and taking from it that you can fool around with drugs and alcohol and get out of it unscathed. You can't.

It's important to understand that ROCKET FUEL is more powerful the more pure it is. Intention, purpose, and commitment will keep you away from substances and activities that weaken your fuel. This is part of the reason I'm obsessed with having a full calendar, with always having something to do, and regularly keeping with my diet and exercise. Whenever I wasn't living with intention and purpose, I went backwards.

From Proactive... To Reactive

I felt I was on the right track from age 11 to 18. I had good grades, played sports, and hustled to give it my all. Things changed when I turned 18 and went off to college. I played football at a small Division 3 college in Maryland. It was the first time I was out on my own and making my own decisions without accountability to my parents. My mom and my stepdad, George, did a great job raising me. They taught me right from wrong, but, when I got to college, I let my focus slip. I was a kid from a small hometown whose eyes were opened to a whole new world. At first it was like being a kid at Disneyworld. I felt like I had been missing out on all this stuff!

Having your eyes opened to new things can be inspiring and help you think bigger, but, without clarity and a healthy purpose, it can also lead you down dark and destructive paths if you're not careful.

I began drinking. Every day became a party. Drinking, drugs, and girls.

Classes and football practice became a non-priority. They were just something to do while I was waiting to party and chase girls again. I was often out all night. There were times at football practices I would doze off while waiting for my turn to run a play. I went from being focused and proactive to being lost and reactive. Instead of living life on my terms, I was living it by default. I had stopped being a leader.

Looking back on that part of my life makes me sick. That is NOT who I am.

Who Am I?

"I'm never drinking again!"

I made this proclamation many times after waking up from a night of partying and heavy drinking. But, the next night I'd find myself back at the local bar, drunk again. I remember one time, staring at the urinal and hating myself. I was thinking, this isn't me.

I knew even before my first drink that this was not what I wanted from life. I've watched many people I love go down this road with terrible outcomes.

Soon the drinking wasn't enough and I started smoking weed. When the weed wasn't enough, I chased something new. On and on the pattern went.

Little by little I continued to trade control of my life for the next thrill.

I kept chasing happiness and never catching it. I had no fulfillment. I was depressed and my anxiety was high.

I was living in dissonance with myself, but I continued because I desperately wanted to feel connection and meaning. I remember feeling so lonely unless I was at a bar or hanging out partying with friends.

I knew I should be accomplishing things I hadn't even started to work on.

Before I started drinking, I had felt I was destined for greatness.

Although I have many great memories, I also have regrets about the wasted years and money and for missing out on opportunities for real connection and meaning.

I went to college happy, focused, and with a clear intention of what I wanted in life.

After two and a half years, I had lost my focus, quit football, and dropped out of college.

Be Prepared. Be Intentional.

Being prepared is the start of being intentional.

Some people go to rehab to recover from addiction.

For me, it was the commitment I made when I met my wife. The first time I saw Jen, I knew I wanted to marry her.

I know it's cliche, but nonetheless, it's the way I felt.

I committed to myself that day to do whatever it took to make that happen.

I committed to removing all obstacles. I didn't blame drugs or alcohol, they weren't the problem. I was the problem. I had lost my focus and my purpose.

When we lose our purpose, we get bored. When we get bored, we look for something to get out of that boredom. When we are bored without purpose, it's easy to turn to things like drugs or alcohol to try and fight the miserable feelings of boredom and being disconnected.

ROCKET FUEL

When I was dating my wife, I remember thinking we needed to go to the bar on the weekends. What else would there be to do? My mind was so conditioned to believe fulfillment came from partying.

It took time to rewire my programming to how much more there is to life.

There is more to life, but it's easy to forget when you dull your purpose and stop living with intention.

Commit to being proactive. If I were able to go back and talk to my 18-year old self, I would remind him that our decisions impact everyone around us. It's a selfish thing to live without intention.

What's At Stake?

Every choice has consequences. Here are some of the things that suffered during the years I let my focus slip. I share these in hopes you might find areas in your life that are suffering from lack of focus. Notice how all these things link together and affect each other.

1. **My Time:** Time is a commodity. We only have so much time. Account for your time. It's been said that you can tell what a person values by looking at their calendar. The activities you do with your time are either leading you towards your dreams or away from them. If the way you're spending your time doesn't match what you believe to be your values, you will never find true fulfillment and joy.

2. **My Diet:** Diet can be a challenge even when you're in the right frame of mind. What you consume is truly fuel for your physical body and it affects everything including how you feel, how you think, and how you act. Do you want your body running like a gummed up engine in a beater car or like a clean, efficient engine in a high powered sports car?

3. **My Self-image and Confidence:** This is an area you can truly use to build massive success. Without it, things become difficult, if not impossible. How you feel about yourself will affect your decisions and your beliefs. It will determine whether you play it safe in life or take calculated risks. It also affects your relationships, career, and finances.

4. My Sleep: I either slept very little or slept a lot at the wrong times. Your mood is determined by the quality and quantity of your sleep. Seven to eight hours per night is crucial to operating at optimal levels. Recovery is a critical piece of success. It's imperative.

5. My Money: Your financial decisions need to be made with a clear mind and with your future in mind. Don't waste your money on meaningless or destructive things. Look to spend your money in areas that will provide you more of the life you truly want.

6. My Production: When you're not in optimal shape with optimal clarity, your potential suffers, as does your ability to perform. If you want to be massively productive, you need to have a base that can support massive production.

7. My Attitude: Living without purposeful intention allows others to be in control. You can't possibly be operating with 100% responsibility. Take control of your life and create a life by design. Stop living in victimhood and blaming others for your circumstance.

8. My Health: We only get one life, and it's short. There is plenty that can hurt you without doing it to yourself. Your survival, and your ability to be your best, depend on how healthy you are. Don't wait to take action on your health.

9. My Mind: Clarity is a must for success. Focus on feeding your mind so you can think clearly, tackle problems, and remember what's important.

ROCKET FUEL

CHAPTER 2

Believe It To See It

"The mind can only perceive what it believes possible to be true."
- James Purpura

Beyond Positive Thinking

I don't want to get too much into the technical aspects of how the mind works in this book. I've shared in this book what works while trying to stay away from why it works. If you'd like to know more about the why, I recommend *Beyond Positive Thinking* by Dr. Robert Anthony. It's the best book I've read on the topic. What I've found in my life is that anytime I didn't have my own purpose or intentions, I lived someone else's. There was never an in-between. When things went the way I wanted, it was because I had set the course. I had pre-determined where I wanted to go, whether I was aware of it or not.

As I've mentioned, my mom always told me, if you believe in something, stick to your guns. I didn't fully understand the concept as a young man. I just knew that when I wanted something, I'd remove any obstacles and do anything I needed to get it done.

I've always gone after everything I want, good or bad, relentlessly. My mom's message has stuck with me to this day.

ROCKET FUEL

People sometimes ask me, "How did you know what you wanted and how did you have the confidence to think you could get it?"

They share their fears, challenges, discomforts, criticisms, and disappointments that they feel are holding them back. Here are some things I've found to be successful in conquering these fears and converting them into ROCKET FUEL.

> *PERCEPTION*
>
> *noun*
>
> *the ability to see, hear, or become aware of something through the senses.*

Based on the above definition, perception is the sensation interpreted by an individual based on experience. Every person has their own perception of every experience. That perception becomes our reality.

To "be real" means that something is acknowledged to be in existence by an individual. If you perceive something to be there, then your mind doesn't know the difference. It just accepts it as reality due to the perceived senses and the context and contrast from your past experiences.

Believe It Before You See It

To accomplish something, it's imperative to believe it before you see it. If you don't, it will limit what you can achieve.

Henry Ford revolutionized the car industry by envisioning and developing the assembly line. Steve Jobs envisioned the iPhone and brought it to life.

Think big, bigger than you think possible. This is how you grow.

Without the ability to imagine something better, you will stay in the same place you are. If you're not focused, you're… blurry!

Have you ever tried to go after something and it feels like you are forcing it? Progress comes slow, or not at all. When this happens, you need to check your belief and faith in what you're trying to accomplish. Chances are, you really don't believe you can achieve the goal.

I'm not suggesting everything will be easy if you envision it first, but, if it feels forced, chances are you need to go back to the beginning and work on clarity and painting the perfect picture of your future reality.

If you don't include chocolate as an ingredient, you won't ever get a chocolate cake coming out of the oven.

Positive Self-Talk

Positive self-talk is the only way that you should be communicating with yourself.

If you're not talking to yourself in the right way, you can't expect others to view you in a positive light. Everything starts with your view of yourself. The following are common negative self talk:

"You idiot!"

"You don't know what you're doing!"

"Why are you always messing up?"

"I can't understand…"

"What's wrong with me?"

Talking to ourselves this way is dangerous. What we say to ourselves, we start to believe. What we believe, we move towards. What we move towards, we project into the world. We will see these beliefs in the words and actions from others. Your life will be exactly what you've determined for yourself. You will see what you always tell yourself.

Here are four steps to improve positive self talk:

Step 1. When you find yourself talking negatively, trigger a response to stop and change course immediately. Say the opposite of what you started to say. Say things like:

"That is not me. I am smart and I just made a mistake."

"I am smarter than that!"

"I know what I am doing."

"I rarely mess up."

"What can I do to understand this?"

"Everything is right with me, I'm happy and healthy."

"I believe I can do that."

Step 2. Start purposefully practicing positive self-talk. Intentionally go overboard and say friendly and encouraging things to yourself.

Step 3. Get others involved. Tell your family, friends, and co-workers about what you're doing and ask them to do it as well. Make it fun and encourage each other.

Step 4. Stay consistent with it and watch it change your trajectory and your life.

Affirmations

You may have heard of the importance of daily affirmations. Few people practice it because of a lack of patience and discipline.

> *AFFIRMATION*
>
> *noun*
>
> *The act of affirming; a positive assertion. To affirm means to state positively.*

It takes consistency to reprogram your mind. You are recreating your reality. The more we can tie our thoughts to emotions, the more successful we will be.

"We think thousands of thoughts every day, but the ones that influence us are the ones tied to emotion. Visualization is the process of taking a thought and keeping it long enough so that our mental picture of it evokes an emotional response. Keep in mind that thought plus emotion creates conviction, and conviction creates reality."
- Dr Robert Anthony

Thought Plus Emotion Creates Conviction

My self-talk sounds like this:

"What are you made of?

You are built for this!

You can handle anything that comes your way!

You are an animal.

Everything You touch turns to gold.

You're an inspiration.

Nothing can stop you!"

Conviction Creates Reality

You're either creating the life you want or you're accepting the life you have. Before I talk about intention statements, understand you are setting intentions whether you set intention statements or not. Your lack of clearly defining your intentions will lead you unintentionally away from the life you want.

You also need to be aware of any counter intentions that might be blocking the intentions you want.

I used intention statements in the past and they didn't work, or at least I thought at the time that they didn't work. What was actually happening was that I was unintentionally hiding counter intentions within my intentions. I was not truly believing my intentions statements because of my underlying beliefs.

In other words, you can say you want something a million times, but, if you don't believe it, you won't achieve it.

Intention Statements

Intentions are like muscles, the more you use them, the stronger they'll become. I say my intentions when I wake up, when I go to bed, and whenever I'm feeling down. As Dr. Anthony recommends, I focus on using words that trigger the feelings and emotions I want.

Here are some of my intention statements that I repeat regularly:

I intend to be great in all that I do, always reaching for my given potential.

I intend to be a loving and supporting father of my children, spending at least 30 minutes with each one per day.

I intend to be loving, supportive, and faithful to my wife, spending at least 60 minutes alone per day with a minimum of one date night per week.

I intend to become the go-to leader on converting setbacks to fuel for high profile entertainers, athletes, and businesspeople, making them feel that I can help them achieve their desired outcomes.

I intend to be in great shape and look fit, weighing 195lbs, lifting weights a minimum of 4 times per week and doing cardio a minimum of 30 minutes three times per week.

I intend to be surrounded by people I admire who are more successful, knowledgeable, and wealthier than I am. This makes me feel uncomfortable and stretches me to avoid complacency.

I intend to learn one new thing per week minimum.

I intend to be raising my targets once they are achieved and shortly celebrated.

I intend to pursue my goals relentlessly and never quit, knowing I can't fail if I keep going after them.

I intend to make $10 million in the next two years.

CHAPTER 1

Blast Off

"Convert your setbacks into ROCKET FUEL to launch yourself to new levels of success and beyond."
- Mike "C-Roc" Ciorrocco

Four Words of Power

I hope you've come to agree that setbacks can be converted into explosive comebacks. In summary, here are four powerful words that have helped me in my journey. I hope they can help you as well.

> *RESPONSIBILITY*
>
> *noun*
>
> *1: the state or fact of having a duty to deal with something or of having control over someone.*
>
> *a: moral, legal, or mental accountability*
>
> *b: reliability, trustworthiness*

ROCKET FUEL

Who's responsible? Believe it or not, it's my responsibility every time. There were times in my past when I blamed another person or situation for something that happened to me, but now I live with the belief of being 100% responsible for my situation and my responses.

If you leave responsibility and control in someone else's hands, you will never accomplish the life of your dreams. Don't wait for someone else to do something with your life. If you do, the life you want will never come. This is why you have to take action now and be 100% responsible.

Be selfish (taking care of yourself), but not self-absorbed (thinking everything is about you). It's your ethical and moral obligation to be responsible and successful.

> *BELIEF*
>
> *noun*
>
> *1: a state or habit of mind in which trust or confidence is placed in some person or thing*
>
> *2: something that is accepted, considered to be true, or held as an opinion: something believed*
>
> *3: conviction of the truth of some statement or the reality of some being or phenomenon especially when based on examination of evidence*

From the moment I first thought about writing a book, I envisioned it would become a bestseller and impact millions of lives. I believe both of these things WILL happen. Whether they happen or not is totally up to my actions. It could happen fast or slow, but, if I'm willing to put in the time, effort, resources, and energy towards it without quitting, it will happen.

There have been times in this process when I've heard the negative voices telling me, "You can't write a book. Why would anyone want to read what you have to say? You'll never get this book finished. No one will buy this book."

I persisted and, not only did I get it done, I sold over a thousand copies before I even completed the book. I'm not special. You can do this too. Believe it and you will SEE IT.

I intentionally choose to spend time around those who help me and support me towards my goals. This, along with my strong belief, helps me beat that negative voice's ass.

STUBBORNNESS

adjective

1a: unreasonable or perversely unyielding: MULISH

1b: justifiably unyielding: RESOLUTE

2: performed or carried on in an unyielding, obstinate, or persistent manner stubborn effort

3: difficult to handle, manage, or treat

I've been stubborn for as long as I can remember. It's been both an asset and a liability at times. Being called, "stubborn" can have a negative connotation. However, it's a good thing to be stubborn about the right things. Be stubborn for your dreams and for the life you want.

In my opinion, being stubborn is a strength and a requirement. It's a must for converting setbacks into ROCKET FUEL and to THRUST you forward towards your goals and dreams.

I love the definition of stubborn being, 'perversely unyielding.' I approach everything I do with this mindset.

RESILIENCE

noun

1: the capability of a strained body to recover its size and shape after deformation caused especially by compressive stress

2: the ability to recover from or adjust easily to misfortune or change

---

ROCKET FUEL

There are a lot of people using the word resilience right now. It's a "buzz word." But, for me, being resilient goes above and beyond the softness most people are using it for right now. Resilience to me means to execute and attack your goals every day. Get back up when you get knocked down.

Whatever the setback, refuse to quit. Sometimes things take longer than wanted or expected. No matter how hard it gets, or how long it seems to be taking, don't quit going after what you want. Action will always get you closer to your potential than if you never try or if you quit.

Be proactive in your resilience and you'll be on the path to UNSTOPPABILITY.

Over a Barrel

There are times in my life when I've felt trapped. Times when I felt that something, a person or a situation, had me "over a barrel."

Before starting my own business, I was in a sales job I hated. At the time, I didn't believe I had the knowledge or the skills to find something better.

It turns out I had everything I needed to go out and find something better. It just took me a while to figure it out.

Another time, when running my business, I felt trapped in keeping highly productive salespeople even when they were bad for our culture. My team and I felt we had to put up with their negative behaviors because we didn't think we could survive without the revenue they were bringing in. It turns out we could.

Being held "over a barrel" means to feel you are in a helpless position; at someone's mercy. When this happens, you give up responsibility and, too the degree you give up responsibility, you give up control.

Two things happen when you give up control.

One is that the blame game starts. Have you ever noticed that when you blame someone or something, it never feels good? It never solves anything. No conflict was settled because of blaming someone or something. If you take responsibility, it diffuses conflict. The wind will be taken out of the accuser's sails. Try it. The next time you're in a situation where there's an argument or conflict at home or work. Take responsibility for what you could have done to contribute to the issue. Be genuine with it. Watch the responses of those around you. Once you see what this does, you'll want to do it more and more. It's a powerful thing.

The second thing giving up control does is it creates a situation of waiting. You're waiting for something to happen or someone to do something. This leads to procrastination. Procrastination causes you to stay in waiting conditions longer and delays your ability to convert the situation into ROCKET FUEL. Quick action is always the best medicine for adversity or setbacks. By taking action, you're immediately opening your mind to see opportunities.

Chose To Do

"The few who do are the envy of many who only watch."

- Jim Rohn

You have a choice in life. You can sit back and watch others while they do, or you can do while others watch.

What is it that causes us to settle? Why do we doubt our abilities? Why do we listen to the negative voices in our heads and from other people?

Throughout our lives, we build a cage of artificial limitations that keep us from living up to our potential. We all do this, there are no exceptions.

Those who succeed in life are those who figure out how to break free from this cage and overcome the negative voices in their lives. They choose to live in growth and abundance.

The truth is, we all also have that voice telling us we CAN do it. Unfortunately, most of us allow the negative voices to have more influence than the positive voices. We live in fear because it's been ingrained in us to "be safe," and to "be normal."

Everything you think, say, and do will either get you closer to your dreams or move you farther away. The key to unlocking the cage of limiting beliefs is to BELIEVE you CAN.

Have you heard the saying, "I need to see it to believe it?" This has never made sense to me. We can only see what we believe, so, if we don't believe it first, we won't ever see it. We need to be intentional with our thoughts and beliefs.

As I've said before, almost everything I've wanted to happen has happened. When things don't happen for me, it's usually because my desires changed with new information or because there's a limiting belief holding me back.

You can do this too!

There are times where it's important to watch and learn, but, at some point, you must take action. The most important part of taking action is the production that comes from it.

No production comes from watching. Too many people get caught up in just observing others.

They either watch in amazement or they watch in envy. Neither of these are productive.

Most people are not conscious they are watchers. They believe they are doers and don't realize they easily become distracted when a real doer comes along.

You Can Do It

Writing this book has been part of an incredible journey. Along the way, I've experienced amazing things happen for me, for my family, and with my co-workers and my business.

When I started my podcast, one of my first guests told me I had no idea what was going to come from what I was doing. He was 100% right. Doing this has brought me more fulfillment than I imagined possible. I've formed incredible relationships with some of the most amazing people on the planet. I've seen incredible things happen for people who are following me and watching me. I've seen many people's relationships improve, incomes double, and overall happiness increase.

Momentum has been building and I'm so excited to see where we go from here.

Join Us

You now have the foundation for what you need to launch into orbit and beyond.

I invite you to IGNITE YOUR ROCKET FUEL!

I invite you to join us on the journey to becoming unstoppable.

I can't wait to hear from you and hear about your successes.

Connect with me on Instagram @mikeycroc and join our community.

Remember, life is too short to not enjoy the journey. Take control. Ignite your ROCKET FUEL, blast off, and become unstoppable!

ROCKET FUEL

About Mike "C-Roc" Ciorrocco

Mike "C-Roc" Ciorrocco is the powerhouse behind the *"What Are You Made Of?"* podcast and creator of the ROCKET FUEL Law.

He is a performance coach, author, dynamic public speaker, visionary and thought leader. He has been featured by Yahoo! Finance as one of the **Top Business Leaders to Follow in 2020** and is on a mission to build people. He is driven to Inspire others and he measures his success on how he is able to help others achieve greatness. C-Roc had a fire lit in him at an early age. That fire has ignited him with a fierce desire to compel people to see the greatness inside themselves using past life events to fuel their fire.

C-Roc has mastered the ability to zero in on the linchpin of an organization and has helped many businesses exceed their initial goals and expectations. He's consumed with the passion to help people break free from the confines of complacency and propel to untapped levels of success.

C-Roc has built a highly successful mortgage division with 3 of his best friends and brother! In 2020 he was named **#1 on the list of Top Mortgage Professionals** by Yahoo! Finance. Along with the mortgage business, C-Roc is a co-founder and partner of a tech company called Blooprinted.

Whether it is his business partners, employees, clients or anyone looking to excel at their business, personal life or develop a winner's mentality, C-Roc is ready for the challenge.

C-Roc currently resides in Ocean City, MD with his wife Jennifer of 18 years and their two children, Nicolas and Sophia.

ROCKET FUEL

C-ROC

www.themikecroc.com

CPSIA information can be obtained
at www.ICGtesting.com
Printed in the USA
BVHW091320140521
607266BV00011B/1522/J